D1132352

Still Doing It

Still Doing It

The Intimate Lives of
Women Over Sixty

DEIRDRE FISHEL

DIANA HOLTZBERG

AVERY

a member of Penguin Group (USA) Inc.

New York

Published by the Penguin Group

Penguin Group (USA) Inc., 375 Hudson Street, New York, New York 10014, USA • Penguin Group (Canada), 90 Eglinton Avenue East, Suite 700, Toronto, Ontario M4P 2Y3, Canada (a division of Pearson Canada Inc.) • Penguin Books Ltd, 80 Strand, London WC2R 0RL, England • Penguin Ireland, 25 St Stephen's Green, Dublin 2, Ireland (a division of Penguin Books Ltd) • Penguin Group (Australia), 250 Camberwell Road, Camberwell, Victoria 3124, Australia (a division of Pearson Australia Group Pty Ltd) • Penguin Books India Pvt Ltd, 11 Community Centre, Panchsheel Park, New Delhi–110 017, India • Penguin Group (NZ), 67 Apollo Drive, Rosedale, North Shore 0632, New Zealand (a division of Pearson New Zealand Ltd) • Penguin Books (South Africa) (Pty) Ltd, 24 Sturdee Avenue, Rosebank, Johannesburg 2196, South Africa

Penguin Books Ltd, Registered Offices: 80 Strand, London WC2R 0RL, England

First paperback edition 2009

Copyright © 2008 by Deirdre Fishel and Diana Holtzberg
All rights reserved. No part of this book may be reproduced, scanned, or distributed in any printed or electronic form without permission. Please do not participate in or encourage piracy of copyrighted materials in violation of the authors' rights. Purchase only authorized editions.
Published simultaneously in Canada

Most Avery books are available at special quantity discounts for bulk purchase for sales promotions, premiums, fund-raising, and educational needs. Special books or book excerpts also can be created to fit specific needs. For details, write Penguin Group (USA) Inc. Special Markets, 375 Hudson Street, New York, NY 10014.

The Library of Congress catalogued the hardcover edition as follows:

Fishel, Deirdre.
Still doing it : the intimate lives of women over sixty / Deirdre Fishel, Diana Holtzberg.
p.   cm.
Includes bibliographical references and index.
ISBN 978-1-58333-320-4
1. Older people—Sexual behavior.   I. Holtzberg, Diana.   II. Title.
HQ30.F57   2008   2008028307
613.9'540846—dc22

ISBN 978-1-58333-353-2 (paperback edition)

Printed in the United States of America
1   3   5   7   9   10   8   6   4   2

BOOK DESIGN BY NICOLE LAROCHE

Neither the publisher nor the authors are engaged in rendering professional advice or services to the individual reader. The ideas, procedures, and suggestions contained in this book are not intended as a substitute for consulting with your physician. All matters regarding your health require medical supervision. Neither the authors nor the publisher shall be liable or responsible for any loss or damage allegedly arising from any information or suggestion in this book.

Some of the names and identifying characteristics of the interviewees featured in this book have been changed to protect their privacy.

While the authors have made every effort to provide accurate telephone numbers and Internet addresses at the time of publication, neither the publisher nor the authors assume any responsibility for errors, or for changes that occur after publication. Further, the publisher does not have any control over and does not assume any responsibility for author or third-party websites or their content.

For our mothers, Irma Bellin Stevens and
Freddie Markowitz, not only for giving us life
but for being models of strong, independent-
thinking women. We honor them with our
enduring love. This book is for them.

ACKNOWLEDGMENTS

We'd like to thank our assistant, Nadia Anderson, who is wise beyond her years and whose dedication and skill were invaluable.

We'd also like to thank our agent, Peter Harrison McGuigan, a man in his thirties who got what we were trying to do and championed our cause.

In many ways we are just the conduit for the voices of the thirty-five women interviewed in this book. We want to thank each and every one of them for so fearlessly opening their hearts and sharing their lives with us.

We'd also like to recognize the handful of experts who generously shared their knowledge.

In addition, we'd like to acknowledge our close friends and our sisters for their support and willingness to talk about the issues we were tackling during the long process of writing this. We couldn't have done it without them.

Finally, this book would never have happened had it not been preceded by our documentary film *Still Doing It: The Intimate*

*Lives of Women Over 65.** We'd like to thank all the people who helped make the film possible, including but not limited to Matthieu Borysevicz, our editor extraordinaire; Jan Rofekamp, Barbara Truyen, and John Nadai of Films Transit International, Inc.; Catherine Olsen, Charlotte Odele, and Diane Rotteau of the Canadian Broadcasting Corporation; Mette Hoffman Meyer of TV2 Denmark; the New York State Council on the Arts, for giving us an initial and crucial grant, and, all the broadcasters around the world and film festival programmers, too many to mention by name, who helped us launch the film.

*For information on the documentary, visit: www.stilldoingit.com.

CONTENTS

When the documentary *Still Doing It* came out, the question arose again and again why—at thirty-seven—had I started a project about the intimate lives of women over sixty-five? The answer is simple. That's the moment I got it—that aging, as a woman in America, is fraught with fear—some of it devoid of reality. I remember the summer. I was actually thirty-six, going on thirty-seven, and my sister, who is three years older than me, was turning forty. She was beautiful, had a compelling career, a great apartment, lots of friends. She lived in New York City, where she'd grown up and wanted to live. But to hear her speak about her upcoming birthday was as if her life would soon be over. The source of her apprehension was obvious. She'd broken up with her boyfriend and as a single woman entering her forties she worried that her romantic/sexual life had already skipped town.

I was also single. And from that vantage point her fear was a little alarming. But it was also strange, somehow disconnected from her real life. True, she wanted children and her fertility was obviously diminishing. But the panic seemed all out of proportion. She was healthy and looked great—in fact, better than ever. And our own mother had met the love of her life at fifty-one, after two divorces.

So I started thinking—obsessing is probably a better word—about what aging was really like for women. And if it were bad at forty, what would it be like at fifty, let alone sixty, seventy, or eighty? Right away, I realized that I had images of women over sixty who were smart and political like Nancy Pelosi and Ruth Bader Ginsburg. It seemed like you could even be creative—there was Joyce Carol Oates, Maya Angelou, and Ruby Dee. But what seemed disturbingly absent was exactly what troubled my sister— the image that as an aging woman, especially, good God, a woman over sixty, you could still be juicy, sexy—someone that other people wanted to—to put it bluntly—fuck.

Our mother, Freddie (featured in the film and in this book), had had a great sex life with her third husband, Sid, but tragically he died of cancer. Years later, she wasn't in a relationship. But still she was nothing like the sweet grandmother depicted in the media. She wasn't having sex, but at sixty-nine she sure as hell wished she were. What were other older women *really* like and what kind of lives were they having? I'd heard rumors of women falling madly and passionately in love after sixty, and I became obsessed with finding them, as well as any other woman over sixty open to talking to me about her sexuality.

What I discovered, quite frankly, blew my mind. It wasn't just that I met churchgoing women who wanted sex but not marriage, women who couldn't keep their hands off each other, and women who were having two and three orgasms a night. It was the energy, the openness, and how frequently the word *fun* came up.

While my friends were worrying about their children and careers, many of these older women were living it up. What started as a personal obsession became a mission to get a portrait of these women out into the world. And halfway into making the film, I had the good fortune to meet Diana Holtzberg, who was as excited as I was. As the executive producer of the documentary, she became another creative source and launched the film into the world. She also initiated the idea of writing this book.

My sister's story took a positive turn as well. She met her husband within a year and gave birth to a daughter four years later. But she's not alone in her dread of getting older and perceiving forty as old. The media routinely tout women in their forties and fifties that way. Yet the average life span of women is eighty, and if we're old at forty then that means we're at the end when we're only halfway through. If we see ourselves as dried up at sixty, we've lost decades of our life.

What makes me outraged is that there is so much in this world that's often worse than the way it's portrayed. War, poverty, early sexual experiences! But here's a situation where the reality is often so much better than what we imagine. In fact, many women I interviewed said age had given them the perspective to grab life by the horns. My decision, at forty, to become a single parent was inspired by knowing so many women over sixty who had met challenge after challenge and come out more passionate and alive.

I've aged, however, since I began. At almost forty-seven, not only have I passed my thirties, but fifty looms in the not-so-distant future. And my awareness of ageism and an encroaching invisibility is no longer secondhand information. I've felt the disconcerting feeling of being looked at in public less and less, of feeling somehow self-conscious about signs of aging. Still, over-all, I feel more joy than I ever have.

And six months ago, as I had heard so many older women talk about, life brought a twist I couldn't have imagined. A fellow filmmaker, fourteen years my junior, called me. I had recently decided I wanted to be with women. She was smart, jaunty, impossibly attractive, but because of her age, my first thought was "What does she want from me?" As we spoke, I kept wondering when she was going to ask me to write her a recommenda-tion or for the name of an editor, but she never did; and before we got off the phone we had a plan for Friday night. Still—despite having met older women in relationships with people twenty, thirty, forty years younger—the idea that this was a date never entered my mind!

Luckily for me, my own mental stereotypes surrounding age were pushed further open and we got together that night. But what I've increasingly come to understand is that there are two parallel tracks occurring for many of us as we age: our true lives in juxtaposition to the cultural image. That disconnect begins around forty, and for many women over sixty that divide is mas-sive. Despite the physical realities of aging, life after sixty (espe-cially in those first two decades) can be intensely creative, sexually fulfilling, and wildly fun. Yet the media almost never choose to depict that.

In the face of our society's youth obsession, we need every opportunity we can to sing the praises of older women and older life. It is my hope that this book will do for others what getting to know the thirty-five women interviewed here did for me—give a reference for the phenomenal adventure that aging *can* be.

For the last twenty-five years my sister Celia has been friends with a woman named Harriet who happens to be thirty years her senior. She's a wild, interesting, highly sexual woman who says whatever she thinks. I had always thought Harriet would be a great subject for a film; I just hadn't yet thought of how to best make it. In March 2002 it was Harriet's seventy-fourth birthday and she invited me to her dinner celebration. I had business plans and so wasn't going to go, but when Celia said, "Harriet wants you to know that a filmmaker is coming to shoot material for a documentary she is making about older women and sex," I immediately said yes.

I work for a company that represents quality documentaries on unique subjects. We also develop a select number of films each year, and I thought a film on older women and sexuality—what a great idea. So this is how I first met Deirdre and began working on the film project *Still Doing It: The Intimate Lives of Women Over 65*. I was thrilled by all the possibilities, and remember telling Deirdre this could be not only a groundbreaking film, but also an incredible book, maybe a TV series about older women à la *Sex and the City,* and a Hollywood film.

My mom was my other pull to this subject matter. She has more interests than any woman I know. From my earliest memories she was a voracious reader, concerned with politics and world events, and loved and went to all things cultural. When we were growing up she adored but couldn't afford couture clothes, so she designed and made them herself. Everyone always commented on how well-dressed she was. And she's still like this today at seventy-nine years old. Unhappy in her marriage, she moved out when she was fifty-three, and remarried happily. I had never seen sexy, vibrant older women like my mother or Harriet portrayed on the screen, and I wanted to. I felt sure others would as well and that a film on this topic would sell like hotcakes.

Completing the documentary, however, was much harder than I had imagined despite the fact we had nine extraordinary, diverse women, all with wonderful stories. Getting U.S. broadcasters to come on board with any funds proved impossible. After two years, we had one arts grant and a broadcaster in Canada and Denmark on board, and were able to get it done without paying ourselves a cent. But even with the finished film to offer, most U.S. broadcasters again passed. I was told the gamut: "Advertisers don't care about reaching an older demographic," "The film isn't for our viewers," "We'll have to cut out too much," "No one wants to watch a film about older women," "A film about older women and sex? Forget about it." One broadcaster told me her boss wouldn't look at it because she didn't want to think of herself as an older woman. Another said a film on older women and sex is more taboo than a film on pedophilia. It was an eye-opening nightmare that revealed both the intense ageism ingrained in our society and the discrepancy between our society's obsession with youth and the fact that women over sixty-five are the fastest-growing segment of our population.

I did end up making a good U.S. broadcast deal with the Discovery Times Channel. The evening it first aired nationwide I excitedly tuned in, and was surprised to see they had cut the racy parts and the one lesbian couple out!

Disappointing, well, yes! But it also fueled my determination and passion. And overall, the film has been well received. It has had a successful film festival career, screening in its entirety throughout the United States at top festivals despite its fifty-five-minute length—when films less than seventy minutes rarely get much festival play. It's also garnered great press and enthusiastic audiences of all ages and races, often half of whom have been men. At our first public screening, a young man of nineteen came up to us to say it really touched him. Several college students and other young people have consistently told us that it gives them hope for their futures, and they want to show it to their friends, siblings, parents, and grandparents. We've received many letters from women and men of all ages. And as of this writing, the film has aired in fifteen countries around the world.

When I started working on the film I was in my early forties. Now I'm at the tail end of my forties. And while a bit flipped out about turning the big five-oh, I probably would have needed to be committed for a while if I hadn't worked on the film and this book, learning about all these amazing women who are ahead of me.

I was the only one of my friends who, after graduating from university, didn't want to soon get married and live in a "home with a white picket fence." The idea of it pushed me over the edge. I instead went to work in Budapest, Hungary, when it was still a Communist country, and then worked in Merida, Mexico. I wanted to travel the world, build a career, partake in cultural events, enjoy time with friends and family, have a boyfriend. Marriage and kids was not part of my vocabulary. So why does it bother me at all that I'm about to turn fifty, given I'm lucky to be alive and healthy and never set out to live a traditional life? Because I have found there is still a stigma for women in their late forties who have never married nor had children. And I don't think there should be. While at this stage, I'd get married if the right man came along—and would consider raising children if he wanted them and could help afford them—I'm still not prepared to marry until I meet a man who I feel I will be happy with long term.

For all the women who haven't yet found their soul mate or chosen a conventional life, or find themselves unhappy in their marriage and want to leave, or are divorced or widowed, and for all those who are happily married or happily single, I'd like us all to be able to continue to explore our sexuality or look for the love of our lives, for however long it takes, without feeling self-conscious about it.

I think that as women age we should continue to perceive ourselves and be perceived as desirable, relevant, and an important part of society. So I am grinning and mostly bearing the impending five-oh without needing to go into hiding, all thanks to my mother and the extraordinary women featured in this book and throughout the world who are living their lives to the fullest no matter what age they are.

1.

HITTING SIXTY WITH A BOOM:
THE NEW OLD AGE

When you see an older woman walking down the street, what do you really think about her? Ask yourself. We're not talking about a forty-year-old woman or a fifty-year-old woman, but a sixty-, seventy-, or eighty-year-old woman with real signs of age. Could you imagine that she and her husband lay in bed that morning having sex and talking about world politics? Or that she just met the love of her life and is exploding with desire? Or that she's thinking of leaving her job and joining the Peace Corps and is feeling more creative, adventuresome, and alive than ever before? Well, if you haven't you're not alone.

Our images of older women—the grandmother, widow, fragile little old lady—are so strongly etched in our minds that we've become blind to the full lives of amazing older women living all around us. We've got no idea what's going on behind their closed doors and consequently have no access to the insights of some of the most sexually experienced women on this planet. Older women are *still doing it*, still loving it, and still getting better at it, "it" being whatever their passion is: from having sex to exploring new ideas to embarking on a creative project. Sharing their neglected stories, *Still Doing It* tells the real and revolutionary experiences of some of today's extraordinary older women.

One of them, Elaine, eighty, from Rhode Island, is a deeply spiritual, churchgoing African-American woman who doesn't have a wrinkle on her face. After her divorce, she worked hard as a nurse to raise her children on her own. She says, with high energy and a twinkle in her eye, "I think society does have a hard time with the fact that I am not only a grandmother but also a great-grandmother and I'm still very sexual. They think, Oh, my God, there's something wrong with her. They just don't think these things go together. I see grandmas, and that's all they are, grandmas. But that's not me. I think I'm a good grandmother and great-grandmother, but there's a part of my life that's still mine, and I'm not ready to give that up."

Of course, not all women over sixty are sexual. Not all younger women are sexual, for that matter. There are older women who report that they never liked sex that much when they were younger and they're just as happy to give it up. And there are women who report they have less interest in sex as they grow older. But as Cornell University gynecologist Dr. Peggy Polanescsky points out, our sexuality ebbs and flows throughout our lives due in great part to our circumstances. "I think some women, for whatever reason, over time, lose interest, but sometimes they lose interest because they stop doing it, or sometimes their husband has prostate cancer or something and it all gets tied into his illness, and you don't have a partner for a number of years. It waxes and wanes, even in younger women it can wax and wane, where couples can go a couple of months and they're just not as interested, and then suddenly everything's back again, depending on what is going on in their lives."

People often ask us where we found the thirty-five women interviewed for this book, insinuating that you'd have to go to the ends of the earth to find them. The reality is that phenomenal older women, those who are in relationships and those who are not, are everywhere. We met Rebecca, sixty, a soft-spoken, elegant woman with a shock of white hair who caught our eye when we sat next to her on a plane. She had just taken early retirement and reinvented herself as a photographer after thirty years in another profession, We spotted Tamara (not her real name), sixty-nine, a graphic artist, in a doctor's office, her attention-grabbing tattoo of her granddaughter's name boldly covering her bicep. We met Lori, eighty, a vivacious, German-born beauty, with an artsy style and the chiseled face to match it, at a party.

Friends marvel that once we found these women they were willing to openly talk about their sex life, exclaiming their mother would *never* talk about her sexuality publicly. It's true that women in their sixties, seventies, and eighties grew up in the 1940s and 1950s, when frank discussion about sex was not exactly encouraged, and many older women today are uncomfortable talking about their sex life. We'd be lying if we didn't say that many women we approached didn't want to participate, even anonymously. But two things must be emphasized: (1) Reticence to divulge intimate details (not unusual among younger women, too) is *not* always a reflection of what is happening privately, and (2) the assumption that older women aren't sexual is actually reinforced by younger people, who not only avoid talking to older women about their sexual or romantic lives but often exclude them from social events, assuming that they wouldn't be interested.

Freddie, seventy-nine, with a great head of red hair and a dry sense of humor, is still a practicing psychotherapist. She reports that even in a therapeutic situation clients often assume they can't talk about their sex life because of her age. She frequently has to bring up the topic so her younger clients see that she's neither uncomfortable nor shocked. Once that wall is broken she reports that clients forget about her age and talk freely. The irony, of course, is that women over sixty were obviously sexual before younger people were born, and many still have very strong sexual feelings, which our ageist society rarely acknowledges. All the women interviewed for this book expressed real joy, even gratitude, at being able to share their feelings about sex and romance, a really important part of their consciousness that most younger people wrongly assume they've outgrown.

PIONEERS

The truth is that there are remarkable senior women everywhere whose irreverence, daring, and sexuality could teach younger women a thing or two. Despite stereotypes to the contrary, they're taking more risks, not fewer, as they age. After a lifetime of worrying about what other people think of them, many frankly don't care anymore. Their awareness of their mortality has made them see just how precious life is. They know what they want, and they're willing to go for it, whether it's letting a potential lover know they're interested or going to Peru to climb

Machu Picchu. Even "traditional" women, like Juanita, seventy-four, a stunning African-American woman with high cheekbones and the posture of a queen, are not willing to be denied what they want and how they want it. A devout Christian who worked as a chambermaid before marrying a much older man who died while her kids were growing up, Juanita doesn't want to remarry. She's unwilling, however, to give up the gratifying relationship and sex life she has with her long-term boyfriend that, outside of marriage, her church considers to be a sin.

THERE WEREN'T OPTIONS

I t's easy to think that many older women were traditional as young women. The majority married young and quickly had children. Those who did engage in premarital sex most often hid the fact. But there weren't the same options women enjoy now: to postpone marriage, live with rather than marry partners, or choose to have children on their own. Instead they had to wait until later in life to make those changes and reinvent themselves to become the women they are today.

Elizabeth, seventy-four, from Pittsburgh, who radiates an inner and outer grace, now enjoys two boyfriends, one for sex and one for his mind. Not the kind of life her strict Christian background prepared her for. "You weren't supposed to have any sexual activity until you were married. Well, it turns out I didn't wait until I got married, but I ended up marrying the first man I slept with. And I thought it was the thing I wanted to do. But I was only nineteen years old, and I thought, Well, maybe I won't find anybody else. I wasn't pregnant when we got married, but I did get pregnant that first month; we were still in college. So right from the beginning it wasn't easy for me to express my sexuality because I didn't want to get pregnant. Even after I was married it was hard for me to go and get a diaphragm. I mean, looking back on it today, it's hard to believe, but that's the way it was in the nineteen fifties. I was embarrassed to go and get birth control. I had two children, and I was still embarrassed."

Penny, eighty-five, a petite, pretty woman with the bearing of someone raised to be a lady, married her husband at "twenty-one or twenty-two." She was from Massachusetts, and he was a Hoosier, so she moved to Indianapolis to be with him. But she soon found that he was not the most loving partner. "I almost felt as though [his work] was his mistress. He was a golfer and a businessman, and I was like someone on the shelf who, if you want to say hi, there I'll be." She thought about leaving him a couple of times, but put everyone's needs before her own. "I couldn't do it because I thought of my two children. It would not be fair to my husband or to my husband's mother and dad. So I came back to Indianapolis. I got involved in a lot of volunteer work. It's what filled in the gaps for me." It would take fifty years, until her husband's death, before Penny would know the joy of a really attentive lover.

Cara, sixty-six, a woman with a dark intensity, is now a lesbian, but she was a devout Mormon as a young woman. She married young and had three children. It wasn't until 1975, when she was thirty-six and moved from her home in Salt Lake City to the more liberal Ann Arbor, Michigan, that she got divorced and came out. "It was the era. I didn't have a lot of options. The older women I admired were married people, and so growing up you dated boys, got married, had children. I was aware of my sexual orientation all the time, but yeah, I repressed it because there was nothing I could do about it. Until probably the 1970s, the American Medical Association still considered homosexuality a mental illness." So Cara married to cover up her secret, ". . . and I wanted children. I wanted a family, and back in those days it was the only way to have a kid."

But as the sexual revolution dawned, women suddenly had more options. Ellen, seventy-four, a former nutritionist whose boundless, kinetic energy still commands, credits the women's movement with giving her the courage to leave a loving, but sexually unsatisfying marriage to live more authentically as an out lesbian. "In high school I had crushes on girlfriends. I remember being madly in love with Gene Tierney in *Laura*. I expect that their mothers caught wind and told their daughters you better not go near that Ellen girl. I felt that I was doing something wrong. I ultimately did get married, but in my late thirties we began to have younger women in the house who helped take care of the children, and by that time I was really ready to make sexual advances. I knew that I had to get a divorce." Ellen's face lights up when she speaks of what the women's movement did for her. "I cannot tell you how lucky I feel to have come out just at the time that the women's movement was exploding," she says. "It legitimized everything I felt. I became alive. I physically became alive." Today she reports her sexual life has the sublime quality of enjoying something that was once forbidden.

According to the U.S. Census Bureau, the percentage of women thirty to thirty-four who were never married practically tripled between 1970 and 2000, reaching 22 percent.

To longtime sexual revolutionaries like Betty, a seventy-eight-year-old sex expert who came of age and into her own in the days of love-ins and key parties, today's young people sometimes seem hopelessly staid. "In the sixties—can you imagine—on Saturday night, instead of sitting around watching television like everyone is doing now, we were at a party having sex with a lot of wonderful people. I mean, how much fun can you have? Well, I can tell you: It's a lot more than we're having now." But even Betty says of getting married at twenty-nine, "It was the nineteen fifties; you had to get married."

While women like Betty and Ellen may be outspoken for their generation, they mark a sea change. Women over sixty-five are the fastest-growing segment of the population. By 2030, 28 percent of the population will be over sixty-five, and two thirds of these will be women. The baby boomers, the largest and most influential generation in American history, started turning sixty in 2006, and as their numbers increase, society is in for a shock. These boomers are women who came of age in the era of free love and flower power, of mass protests and bra burning, of birth control and sexual experimentation, and they're not about to throw in their wild-child ways when they sign up for Medicare. These movers and shakers will not settle into sexless obscurity, satisfied with merely living longer; they want to have fun, too. And with the average life span of American women already pushing eighty, sixty can be just the beginning of a whole new chapter. As futurist Maddie Dychtwald, sixty, says, "As we live longer, reinvention is going to be the key." Just picture it: Seniors buying sex toys, gay-friendly nursing homes, and women not only finding the loves of their lives in their seventies and eighties but also getting into alternative relationships, switching careers, following their creative and sexual desires. Yet despite the fact that there are already groundbreaking older women out there and we are on the cusp of a revolution, the image of older women as sexually dried up is still pervasive.

A LITTLE HISTORY LESSON

The truth is, older people, and especially older women, have always been more sexual than society has been prepared to accept. This stubborn streak of denial seems to run especially deep in the United States, which has a long, troubling history of denying women's sexuality dating back to (not surprisingly) the Puritans. At a time when accusations of witchcraft in Europe and elsewhere were being met increasingly with doubt and acquittals, in colonial Massachusetts older women were still being hanged as witches largely because of their overt sexuality or positions of power.

At the center of the Salem, Massachusetts, trials was Tituba, the Arawak native who was sold to Reverend Samuel Parris, and was believed to be his concubine and mother of his child. Then there was Bridget Bishop, who was approaching sixty and just five years into her third marriage when she was accused of witchcraft. Clearly, these sexually active, strong-minded older women were more than the Puritans were prepared to tolerate. Ruth, seventy-two, a wisecracking, superathletic psychologist, says, "When they were burning witches at the stake in the fifteenth, sixteenth, and seventeenth centuries most of these were older women who were viewed as dangerous in terms of sex and sexuality, and I think there was a sense that men, the male hierarchy, felt threatened."

Science has quelled accusations of witchcraft in the interven-ing centuries, but it hasn't eradicated society's fear of women's sexuality. As Joyce, a documentary filmmaker and psychologist with an easy manner that invites comfort, says, "If we accept that women are sexual after their childbearing years, we have to admit that their sexuality is not about bringing in the next generation but about unabashed joy and pleasure." But as the brief fad of female circumcision in this country in the 1860s for cases of nymphomania or intractable masturbation* attests, unabashed joy and pleasure were clearly not what society wanted women to enjoy.

Dr. Alfred Kinsey, however, took bold steps toward sexual understanding with the establishment of the Kinsey Institute for Sex Research. His 1948 publication of *Sexual Behavior in the Human Male* was greeted as a medical breakthrough and went on to sell hundreds of thousands of copies. However, an international media storm greeted his 1953 follow-up on women's sexuality, which reported that women were masturbating, having sex before they married, and, yes, being sexually active even as grandmothers. The study was widely hailed by fellow scientists but immediately prompted denunciations by pastor and presidential advisor Reverend Billy Graham, which eventually led the Rockefeller Foundation, Kinsey's key patron, to withdraw its financial support for his research.

LIVING LONGER, HAPPIER, SEXIER LIVES

As the century progressed, however, research in support of Kinsey's findings began to accrue. In the 1960s, gerontolo-

---

*Documented in Barbara Ehrenreich and Deirdre English's legendary book *For Her Own Good.*

gist Dr. Ruth Weg began her lifelong study of the sexuality of older women. In 1975 she initiated her pioneering program "Sexuality and the Whole Person," which included a then-revolutionary discussion of "alternative lifestyles for independent adults (homosexuality, bisexuality, polygamy)" that led to the eventual establishment of the American Society on Aging's (ASA) Lesbian and Gay Aging Issues Network. Dr. Weg's subsequent book, *Sexuality in the Later Years: Roles and Behavior,* first published in 1983, put sexuality on the map for gerontologists and those working with older adults. In 1980 the then-fifty-two-year-old Dr. Ruth Westheimer created a sensation with a fifteen-minute radio segment called "Sexually Speaking," which championed sexual literacy among women and men of all ages. Her openness about sexuality was embraced like a breath of fresh air.

The publication of Kinsey's Sexual Behavior in the Human Female also prompted a follow-up poll of 1,000 women between the ages of eighteen and fifty by The People, a London tabloid, which primly concluded: "British women are much more moral, more conventional, and more faithful to the marriage bond than the American women of the Kinsey Report." Obviously fear of women's sexuality is not only an American hang-up.

These medical pioneers made deep dents in our puritanical notions of age, yet incredibly the stereotype of the worn-out, sexless older woman has followed us into the twenty-first century. Dr. Christina Puchalski, an internist at George Washington University Hospital in Washington, D.C., reports that she "has to laugh when I do a sexual history with my older patients and I have a medical student in the room. They're just in shock that people have sex after sixty-five."

Fifty years after Kinsey, ageist stereotypes continue to strait-jacket older women. Sadly, many older women themselves, who can't help but be affected by pervasive ageist assumptions, initially find it surprising that they still feel sexual. As Elaine, who has come to accept that she is a great-grandmother who likes sex, told us, "I found that I had these yearnings, and at first I thought, Oh, God, you're much too old for this. But then I thought, Why would I be having these feelings if my body were too old?"

ADVERTISING

It's not surprising that many women feel the way Elaine does. There are so few images of and stories about women over sixty being sexual. A major culprit is the billion-dollar advertising industry, whose purchase of air time largely determines television programming. Unfortunately, it still uses a model from the Depression era that assumes that older people are so rigid and have so much brand loyalty that the brands they choose are fixed in stone. Of course, how many older people do you know who wouldn't be open to trying a new toothpaste, a new brand of sneakers, or a new car for that matter? But real or not, if advertisers perceive they can't make money from a particular demographic, they're not going to finance projects geared to that group. Maddie Dychtwald, whose work concentrates on issues relating to older women and business, says perhaps, "it's because the average age of the buyers is twenty-eight. . . . Whatever the reason, it's clearly rubbish. In fact, sixty percent of the wealth in this country is in the hands of people over fifty." What makes this preconception particularly perverse is that the advertising industry is actually losing money because of it. But even an over-sixty CBS senior executive, David F. Poltrack, who wants to create programming for older audiences, recently declared at New York's Women in Film and Television that the ageist biases in the advertising industry still work against what he's able to bring to the screen.

A few smart people, however, are not willing to simply accept this antiquated reasoning. In 2006 acclaimed indie director Susan Seidelman made *The Boynton Beach Club*, a film about a woman in her sixties dating. The response she got from distributors was predictable: "It's a nice movie, but we don't believe there's enough commercial potential in that demographic," Seidelman recalled. "That didn't compute for me. I'm over fifty, and I go to the movies at least once a week. My mother is over seventy, and she goes twice a week. My sixteen-year-old son barely goes at all; he's online all the time. I think people over fifty are the most underrepresented audience."* In order to prove her point Seidelman engineered a limited release in South Florida and Palm Springs, California. The huge numbers of people who showed up to see the film got it theatrical distribution in 2006 with Roadside Attractions in the United States and a worldwide release. Eric d'Arbeloff, co-owner of Roadside Attractions, told us, "There's no question the older audience reliably goes to movies, yet for the most part they're ignored by the studios. So they represent an opportunity for independent distributors like us, as we discovered on our successful releases of *Ladies in Lavender* and *Boynton Beach Club*. Still, the older audience is not without its challenges:

*Stephen Farber, "Hollywood Awakens to the Geriatric Demographic," *The New York Times*, July 2, 2006.

They tend not to come out on the first weekend, which is tough because the theaters give us so little time. Second, they don't buy or rent DVDs the way younger people do, and this is where the profit in the business is now made."

Clearly audiences (largely older but also younger) are hungry for film and television that portrays older lives, particularly those with romantic/sexual themes. But the fight to make the mainstream media aware that older life is something audiences are going to pay to see is still far from over.

In the last few years we've begun to see a handful of titillating older women in the movies. Witness Helen Mirren in *Calendar Girls*, Diane Keaton in *Something's Gotta Give*, Charlotte Rampling in *Heading South*, Susan Sarandon in *Alfie*, and Barbra Streisand playing a senior sex therapist married to Dustin Hoffman in the hit *Meet the Fockers*. But these characters are still only in their late fifties or early sixties. The image of women in their mid to late sixties, seventies, and eighties who are sexually vibrant is still largely absent, even taboo.

What's so sad is that not only are older women being denied images of sexuality and romance that reflect their reality, but the rest of us aren't seeing the joy our later years can bring. We're so inundated with the image of sex as two hot pumping young bodies that even thinking of women in their seventies and eighties having sex seems foreign, if not distasteful.

If you go on the Internet and look up "older women and sexuality," it's shocking how little is there. And what there is is mostly porn sites with names like "SEXUALLY EXPLICIT: Granny Goes Wild!" The message is clear: Women over sixty having sex is a joke. And since most of us, if we're lucky, are going to reach that age, the joke ultimately will be on us.

But whether it's been documented or not, the truth, and what we should all be shouting from the rooftops, is that the reality of older women's lives is a hell of a lot better than the images we're exposed to. And psychological, sociological, and medical data overwhelmingly prove it. Despite what popular culture leads us to believe, the National Institutes of Health report that 80 percent of women experience mild or no menopausal symptoms. For some women, the increased levels of testosterone that come with menopause actually increase their sexual appetite. Harriet, a well-read seventy-nine-year-old bohemian with a head of long, flowing white hair and an irreverence that charms many and alarms a few, declares, "After menopause your whole hormonal structure changes, and you become much more sexual. I mean, it's something that women are really being confused about, and it's being hidden from them, I think. . . . First of all, the psychological factor that you don't have to worry about getting knocked up is a big factor. And second of all, that testosterone thing just gets you hotter all the time. You have to balance it with estrogen, otherwise you'll grow a beard or something [laughs], but it's great. Sex is getting better all the time . . . and I feel very much part of that thing, the freedom of it. I feel great."

Betty, seventy-eight, also met menopause with zest. Showing us a picture of herself in dominatrix attire that was taken when she was already in her fifties, Betty says, "After menopause I thought, It's supposed to be all over. . . . *Hmmmm,* I don't think so. I think I'll get into some kinky stuff. I've never done that before."

Betty's response to menopause may be radical, but it's not uncommon for postmenopausal sex to improve. First there's the wonderful spontaneity of not having to worry about using birth control (where people know their partners and ideally have been tested for HIV and other sexually transmitted diseases). And despite all the hoopla around how painful the empty nest is, many older women report that it actually gave their sex life a boost. It makes sense that not having to keep an ear open for a crying toddler or worry that a teenager will hear you moan can do more than a little to encourage sexual experimentation. And if you're retired, the luxury of having sex in the morning or afternoon and not just when you hit the pillow already exhausted is obviously another boon to lovemaking.

Just getting older and coming into one's own can have a profound effect on a woman's sexuality. We don't live in a culture that teaches us about it. We're all just supposed to know what to do. But most of the women interviewed told us they didn't know what they wanted sexually when they were younger and if they did they were often too afraid to ask for it. Many said maturity and sexual confidence have made them more comfortable with letting go and seeking their own pleasure. Dell, eighty-four, a woman with an intense gaze and the willowy body of a dancer, started Eve's Garden, the first sex boutique geared for women, in New York City in the 1970s. She says of her sexuality now, "For me it only gets greater as I get older. And I feel it's a factor of liberating myself in a psychological way as well, dropping the trappings of constraint because when you get older you feel, well, this is it. You know, you don't want to cover up anymore. I am freer and less fearful and just more open to what life has to offer, and that's reflected in my sexual nature."

So if women are living longer, healthier lives and remaining open to the possibility of romance and vibrant sexuality as they age, why do we persist in thinking of older women not as enjoying their maturity but (as one cosmetics commercial declares) "fighting it every step of the way"? Much of the answer lies in the money to be made from making women fear the aging process.

As Lois Banner, a cultural historian at the University of Southern California, explains, "Society persists in seeing aging in terms of loss rather than benefit, because capitalism is invested in this vision of its aging people. Capitalism is modeled on the idea of constant change, of what is new. Therefore to look on aging people as becoming better instead of becoming deficient would be to fundamentally challenge the way the whole system is organized and structured. And I think it's going to get worse and worse because there's so much money to be made from it."

According to the American Society for Aesthetic Plastic Surgery, there was a 44 percent increase in the number of plastic surgeries performed in the United States in 2004. Some findings conclude that women feel pressure from ageism on the job to undergo cosmetic surgery. As Ruth, whose day-long bike rides and yoga make her look far younger than she is, says of looking for a job as a research psychologist at sixty-three, "So maybe I didn't look sixty, but I surely didn't look forty or fifty, and I know I didn't get certain jobs because of it."

The billion-dollar cosmetics industry, in fact our whole culture, is built on the premise that old age needs to be fixed. And despite how older women really perceive themselves, most are deeply affected by the feeling that they're "over the hill." Almost every woman we interviewed, no matter how enlightened or sexually active, told us that she feels invisible when walking on the street. As two women in our forties, we have already begun to feel it. As we approach fifty, it's hard not to be filled with some trepidation, despite knowing so many women who hit their stride in the fifth and sixth decades of their lives.

But ageism is a prejudice like any other, full of misconceptions, fears, and stereotypes. In opening our eyes to this culture's perverse and pervasive youth obsession hopefully we can empower ourselves to be bold and feel good at any age. For older women who buy into society's notions of what they "should be like" feel self-conscious, but older women who call their own shots and believe in themselves (while not being immune to that self-consciousness) lead happier, healthier, more fulfilling lives.

It's been over forty years since Dr. Ruth Weg reported her eye-opening findings that "if we've been orgasmic as young women, we will only become more so as we age." And if we can keep having (and wanting) sex, then it makes sense that we don't have to lose other aspects of who we are. So if you've always loved to dance the night away, you'll likely still want to cut a rug when you're older, and if you've always had a quick wit and enjoyed snappy repartee, why assume you'll change? Many women actually become sharper, funnier, and more outspoken as they age.

Our bodies do need care over time. You may be able to get away with eating badly and not exercising regularly when you're in your twenties or thirties, but in your sixties that can make the difference between feeling really good and really sexual and having a host of aches, pains, and other physical problems. Even some women who do take good care of themselves eventually face debilitating pain in their knees or hips that requires surgery or replacement. But our bodies can continue to rejuvenate. And with a little determination and a commitment to eating well and exercising our bodies, we can stay strong and agile. Marnie, seventy-five, a very handsome woman from Minnesota whose thirty years of teaching aerobics has resulted in energy to spare, had a knee operation and then went on to rank in the national skiing finals for her age group. Her body not only looks great, but she's stronger than most people half her age.

Even health can't protect us from the losses that life and aging bring. Every woman we interviewed had experienced the death of a spouse, sibling, or good friend, and many are cancer survivors. But, paradoxically, many told us that grieving and ultimately coping with losses made them more resilient and more eager to experience whatever life has to offer. In fact, many older women find that being closer to the end of their lives than to the beginning makes them more open, more compassionate, more willing to take chances. They are, as cultural critic Dr. Morganroth Gullette describes it, "declining to decline," opting instead to let loose and live large.

Older women are reinventing themselves as they age, not just getting older but coming into their own. In the next eight chapters we'll be exploring the lives of women over sixty from across the country and from every socioeconomic situation: partnered, single, gay, straight, black, white, Latina, religious and not. We'll look at their romances, struggles to find romance, sexuality, and relationship with their bodies. We'll explore their experience of ageism, their losses, and their ongoing drive for adventure, romance, and growth.

While the culture at large persists in seeing older women as staid, prudish, and traditional, there are easily as many young men and women who fit that bill. With boomers on board, the time has come to stop associating older women with rocking chairs and knitting needles; there are fascinating, passionate older women all over the world who are nothing like Whistler's mother.

So what's sex got to do with the age revolution? Sex is so much more than a physical act; it's a metaphor for life itself, an expression of vitality, connection, and joy. Women over sixty are clearly not having sex to procreate, but they *are* having sex. Acknowledging this reality means coming to terms with the fact that women of all ages might have sex simply because they *like* it. And if women are having sex because they want to, what other desires might they pursue in every aspect of their lives?

There are incredible, sexual, energetic older women all over the world, and we're going to tell you about some of them. If you are a young or middle-aged woman today and you're afraid that as you age your life will be over, it's time to stop worrying and start thinking about what you want to do, what you want to accomplish. If you're sixty+ now and are in a rut, it's time to reinvent yourself, find new things to be passionate about. We're all on this earth for a relatively short time. So why waste a precious moment of it? Older life can be fabulous, and women of all ages who don't know this are not alone. We don't pretend that being seventy is the same as being thirty or forty nor deny that aging comes with inevitable difficulties, but the reality is that there are slews of older women out there having the time of their lives. Old age was never what most people thought it was, and it's undergoing the most radical transformation it ever has. Now that the boomers are coming of age, the time of reckoning has arrived. If we can celebrate this part of our later lives, perhaps we can begin to understand that age isn't a numbers game, and birthdays aren't for counting. It's not about the candles; it's about the cake. *¡Viva la revolucion!*

2.

GOING STRONG:
ROMANCE THROUGHOUT LIFE

We are encouraged to think that life follows a specific trajectory. You can enjoy sex and romance while you're young, but this won't last forever. Heat and passion cool with age. If you haven't found someone by forty or fifty you're screwed—or not screwed, as the case may be. Luckily life presents us with some surprises. Passionate, skin-tingling, stomach-jumping romance can happen at sixty-eight and at eighty, sometimes even after we've given up.

Ruth married early and was divorced in her thirties. As the single mom of three kids it wasn't easy for her to focus on finding a partner. But when she was in her fifties, her kids moved out. She got her Ph.D. in psychology, was playing on a softball team, and was feeling great about herself. She wanted to find a man to have a relationship with. She went to bars and answered ads in the *New York Review of Books*, trying to meet someone. Ruth remembers a date with a guy who seemed wonderful on the phone. Her son, Michael, dropped her off "and he was all hopeful because, you know, I think my kids at that point wanted me to get together with a guy. . . . So we had lunch, and all he talked to me about was his ex-wife and how she was raking him over the coals for money. So he was gonna show her. He stopped working; he took a sabbatical; he disposed of his income so she couldn't get anything. . . . So that was the end of him." Ruth told us she had more than her share of dates from hell but still wasn't about to give up. "I was feeling that I had a lot to offer, sexually and personally, career-wise, and so on and so forth."

A few years later, "I met this guy. I really flipped over him. His name was Tom. I think we went to bed on the second date, which is, you know, always a no-no. I really went nuts over him, and we did date for a while and I had this feeling, gee, I would like him to move in with me, which was rather shortsighted but . . . I wrote poems to him, and oh, Jesus Christ, I was really fit to be tied. Anyhow, he did not react in a similar fashion to me. And I was really upset when I made a number of phone calls and he didn't respond, and so, you know, I had to stop. And that was very, very disappointing." Ruth continued searching, but nothing came of it. "Looking back, I don't think that any of my efforts really were fruitful or any of them resulted in any extended dating with any guy."

But in her early sixties Ruth realized it was only going to get harder, so she decided to make a last-ditch effort to get together with someone. Reading the personal ads, she discovered that men ten years older than she were looking for women ten years younger. Over the phone men were more interested in finding out her hair color than her interests. But she responded to a personal ad that sounded interesting: *sixty-four, former statistician, athletic, academic, likes to read.* They set up a date, and because this guy had poor night vision she agreed to pick him up at his house.

Ruth vividly remembers driving up the street and seeing her date for the first time, standing in the driveway. "He had to be a hundred pounds overweight. He had this huge gut. He had on ten-dollar sneakers from Kmart and polyester pants." She went out to dinner with him, but as she drove away she said to herself, "That's it. No more! I'm not going to look anymore. I came in single; I'm going out single. There's not going to be any more sex except with myself, and that's it." It wasn't her first choice, but she was relieved to think she was finally freeing herself from future disasters. "After that date I had such emotion, but in that moment I sort of rid myself of all the looking and the need, and I was happy. I felt complete, and I was satisfied. I didn't have that drivenness to find a man, to look for a man. And three or four months later I met Harry, my husband."

They were introduced through a friend. Everything about getting together with Harry was effortless. Ruth was completely caught off guard. For their third date they planned a weekend biking trip and made reservations at a bed and breakfast along their route. It was clear to her that after a long dry spell that she was going to get laid. "I was nervous. I thought, What am I supposed to do? Is it appropriate? Should I undress in front of him?" Ruth went into the bathroom and took off everything but her underwear. Despite her awkwardness the night was better than she could have imagined. "We just kind of jumped into bed. And then once it started, you know, once he touched me and we hugged and kissed, everything went on from there. Those next two nights were, you know, I'm sure partly because I had been abstaining for all of those years; it was the most! I mean, I was shocked. I think I had two or three orgasms every night. I think Harry was a little blown away, too. And I thought, my God, it was really wonderful. It was just so exciting, and he was obviously very pleased, I'm sure, because he had an erection, because he gave me so much pleasure, and because here I was, you know, whooping it up.

"I think that I went through a period of a month or two at least where I couldn't believe how lucky I was. I almost felt like "Do I deserve this?" I couldn't believe that I had met someone who was my age, a man who wanted a woman his [age] . . . We knew the same songs; we had similar political interests; we liked music, biking, and canoeing and hiking. I was in disbelief."

Ruth felt wild and carefree. She laughed out loud. She'd always loved sex, but her whole experience of sex was different now. "I can't ever remember laughing in bed in any kind of a sexual encounter with my first husband or anyone. Not that it wasn't enjoyable or nice, or I didn't love my partner or he wasn't a great sex partner, whatever, but things are funnier now because I'm much more comfortable with myself. I'm much more comfortable with my sexuality, and there aren't all of these ideas and conditions and morals hanging over me. It is much more natural, and natural things can be funny. That's the best part of sex now. It's funny and fun."

They met in October and were married in February. "I decided to get married in my sixties . . . first of all, he proposed. But there were financial reasons that pushed us to get married as opposed to shacking up and living together because I needed to have more income. And I was on a search for a full-time job with benefits, but my husband wanted me to stop the search so I could spend some time with him. And I couldn't do it financially. It's like either/or. Either we have to do this and join financial empires, so to speak, or I have to go out and get a full-time job. I think this is a predicament that many older women have. They don't have the resources that many older men do. I think that certainly women who have been single for a long time have financial straits that men don't have. So while he proposed and loved me and I loved him and we fell in love and we had this compressed dating and courtship period, the actual marriage was certainly largely a financial decision."

CELEBRATING LIFE

Connie, eighty-one, a professor of anthropology with the classic features of a movie star, married her longtime boyfriend, Antonio, after nine years of being with him. Connie's first husband died when she was sixty, and Antonio, seven years her junior, had been a friend of theirs. After nine years of living with Antonio, they were still enjoying a fiery, sexual relationship, their lives, children, and grandchildren already meshed. "So why did we decide to get married? Actually, many reasons. We had off and on talked about it as simply a celebration of our having lived together for nine years. And feeling very lucky, feeling committed in a way that we had not in our previous relationships. Also very important is the fact that both of us within the past three years had life-threatening illnesses, and so we wanted some way to celebrate, to celebrate life, to celebrate our lives, our lives together. . . . We had earlier decided that it wasn't necessary to get married, that we should just live together. But after these threats, the whole sense of how fortunate we are to have each other and how fortunate it is to live and to make the most of the time that you have for living, to celebrate it, that's when we decided to create a ritual." So on a glorious summer day, with their dearest friends, children, grandchildren, and former students gathered around them, and Connie's dress whipping in the wind, they said, "I do."

This marriage feels very different to Connie than her previous one. "What has changed in this relationship is that I do not require of Antonio what I needed as a younger woman growing up. I assume that's true for him, too. So the relationship doesn't have some of the particular stresses and strains of growing up together and the conflicts and problems you face. It's not that life doesn't have stresses, but I don't ask the same things of my partner; I don't need the same things."

Despite the fact that it was life-threatening illness that ultimately motivated them to get married, Connie says she is still open to whatever life has to offer. "All the time when I go swimming, when I go boating, when we celebrated our marriage, I feel ageless is the way I would put it. I don't walk around feeling old. In fact I'm sometimes surprised when I catch a view of myself in the mirror (and realize, yes, I am old). . . . When I think about why I feel as good as I do right now, apart from having Antonio as a partner, apart from having our children and our grandchildren, apart from having a really wide circle of friends, it is that I have this anticipation, always wanting and being open to something in the future that will be different. I still have that. I still feel connected to life."

NEVER TOO LATE

Frances, eighty-six, whose elegance and sharp wit seem to defy the fact that she lives in a nursing home, has always been passionate about her writing and her relationships. At sixty, after many years of being unhappy, she asked her husband of thirty years (and father of her two kids) to leave, but she soon found that she really missed having a man in her life. Her son Bill said, "Mom, you're a risk taker. Put a personal ad in the *Bay Guardian*." "And so I did. It was a very small ad with no flowery stuff in it at all. It just said, "Sixty-two years young, retired professional woman."

She met a rancher. Even though his life on the ranch was nothing like her urban one, she embraced the experience and lived with him, and they had a wonderful sexual life until he died ten years later. At seventy she found another man with whom she was "delighted to enjoy sex." Then, she says, "At eighty I met a man with whom I am in love. For the first time I am really in love."

Frances began losing her sight in her sixties and was legally blind by her late seventies but in her inimitable way turned this experience into something positive, writing a book about it, *Dancer in the Dark*. It was through her book that she met her lover, David. "A friend said, 'I'll send a copy of your book to David Steinberg, who writes for the *Examiner*, and his column is called Seniorities. Maybe he will review the book.' I did then receive a phone call from David, to say, 'This is an interesting book. It's well written. You have a typo on page seventeen. In my column I can't review the book, but I can interview you as an older person who's active.' 'Fine,' I said, 'that would be just fine.' And he called me several times so that we began to understand each other, and he finally said to me one day over the phone, 'Are you cute?' I said, 'How the hell would I know if I'm cute? I'm blind.' David decided to schedule another interview in person to find out. When she met him at her front door he said, "You are cute. I think I'll kiss you." And so he did. "What do you think I said to him then? I said, 'Lower, a little lower, please.'"

Meeting David, "a man of letters," satisfied her body and mind in ways she'd never experienced before, an extraordinary turn of events for someone with eighty years of life behind her. For Frances the most significant part of their meeting was the sense of familiarity she experienced immediately. "When he came up to the top of the steps and he came around and kissed me, I knew I had come home. I didn't need any explanations at all. I was coming home finally after all the years and all the experiences I've had. I was finally home. And he felt the same way."

Frances had had a lot of lovers and was hardly pining away for another, thinking she'd been missing something in her life. But once she met David she soon realized that this robust eighty-two-year-old with a hearty laugh was everything she'd ever wanted in a man. "I'm in love with David Steinberg. David is the man I should have married when I was very, very young because David is a man of letters, and I believe from that point of view that David is the great love of my life."

When Frances was eighty-two, she had to go into a nursing home because of a broken hip. "In coming to the home here I was the one who made the decision. I had broken my hip and at the same time I had a gallbladder operation, and I was in a most uncomfortable position. I was hurting, hurting badly, and my granddaughter and my daughter were here, both of them very close to me, staying with me just about day and night, where I live, and they didn't know what to do. I said, 'You don't have to. I already solved this problem twenty-five years ago. I told them I had applied to this Jewish home, saying, 'I'll be coming. I don't know when, but I'll be coming.' And every year the intake person would call and say, 'Are you ready this year?' 'No, I'm not ready this year.' 'Alright, I'll call you next year.' Well, that took twenty-five years, and then I said to Christine and Amy, 'No problem. Call up the Jewish home. They're waiting for me.' And that's how I came here. Because I solved my problem way, way, way ahead of time. You look ahead of time, see what your options are, and begin to act on them."

Incredibly, Frances and David's relationship thrived intellectually, emotionally, and sexually even after she moved into the nursing home. We asked Frances if she was surprised that David stayed with her. She immediately replied, "I would have been very disappointed in him if he had walked away from me just because I broke my hip and became impossibly, impossibly unable to take care of myself. That would have been the measure of a person not worth knowing." Despite her frailties, which include not only being blind but also needing assistance walking, Frances has a joyous sense of herself, her sexuality, and her desirability that many of us, younger and able-bodied, can't equal. It's a quality David finds irresistible. When we asked him what attracted him to Frances so strongly, he told us, "There are a lot of available older women out there, believe me. But the answer to your question is, She's Frances. I can't say anything more than that. She's Frances."

They were lucky because the San Francisco Jewish Home for the Aged is a cutting-edge nursing home, and the staff is sensitive to and respectful of its residents' sexuality and need for privacy (which is not always the case elsewhere). Frances describes how she and David shut the door and can escape from their surroundings through physical contact. "The times I have sex nobody matters. I'm in my own world. David is in his own world. We are in our world, and we don't give a damn."

And it's truly amazing to see David and Frances in a room together. Their sexual energy is palpable. We filmed them for our documentary *Still Doing It*, and audiences were astounded that their sexual connection as they held each other was not just sweet but hot. David playfully grabs Frances's bottom. She laughs boisterously, in love with this man and her life. Perhaps that's why Frances never regrets having met him so late. Or maybe it's just her nature. As she says, "I go from one experience to the next, to the next, and within each one take the best I can from it."

COMING OUT

Since there are few stories like Frances's being told in the mainstream media most of us just assume our romantic/ sexual life will be over way before we hit eighty, but where the mind goes, the body will always follow. In her mid-sixties, Dolores, now seventy-five, a mother and grandmother who divorced her husband and had a closeted lesbian relationship in her forties and fifties, moved to New York City from the suburbs. She was thrilled at the prospect of her new life, eager to start school again, to go to the theater, and live in the heart of a city she used to just visit. She hadn't had a lover in years, but she just assumed that "once you've had grandchildren and you're in your sixties it's all over." So it never occurred to her that she might meet another lover. A mutual friend thought Ellen, now seventy-four, could show Dolores around and introduce her to some like-minded gay women, but it was Ellen herself who captivated Dolores, who wasn't at all prepared for the feelings that Ellen sparked in her. "I was just amazed that I even felt like going to bed with somebody because it had been a long time. But when I realized that there was a tremendous amount of desire on my part I seized the moment, and there was never ever any fear. It was just exhilarating. It was fabulous. It was great." It quickly became the most passionate sexual relationship of her life.

While Dolores used to think her chances for romance were over, now she realizes that age is the factor that's let her connect with Ellen in ways she never has before. "Meeting somebody in my middle sixties was the most incredible experience in my life, and I don't think either myself or Ellen would have had this kind of relationship unless we had lived the lives we've had." Ellen also attributes the intensity of their relationship to age and experience. She knows there's no time to waste. "There's almost a keen awareness of the lack of time, and it gives an urgency in being close to someone. It plumbs my depths."

When Ellen met Dolores, she was still getting over a recent breakup. She hadn't given up on ever having sex again in the way that Dolores had, but she was so hurt she assumed she'd never have another significant love. "I ended a relationship, or I would say a relationship ended, in my mid-sixties, and at that point in my life I had a sense of, what time do I have left? I think an acute awareness of being alone overtakes you in the later years, and certainly the ending of a relationship that had been built around the idea—and I really believed was going to last throughout my whole life—was devastating. There was a disillusionment and a deep-rooted hurt that I don't think I had ever experienced in other breakups."

"So what was it like meeting a new lover being in my late sixties? I can tell you it developed into something that I never, never would have dreamt of. I never in a million years would've anticipated that I would meet someone who was not only a companion but who absolutely ignited my life physically, who turned me upside down and on my heels, which I hadn't experienced since I'd been in my thirties. I still sit back and marvel at having that capacity and having a relationship that can do that."

Dolores says, "Most people walking down the street would never in any way, shape, or form, in their wildest dreams, ever think that two seniors well past sixty-five could have a sexual relationship or indeed enjoy it or indeed have anything to do with sex. That's basically what everybody thinks, and it couldn't be further from the truth."

On the one hand, there's something deliciously exciting and forbidden about knowing that everyone just sees you "as two old ladies" and that they have no idea that when you touch hands it means much more than friendship. But Ellen and Dolores also wish younger people knew what was possible for them. Ellen says, "If you'd told me five years ago that my sexuality, my physicality would broaden, would explode, would be deeper and more intense than ever before, I never would have believed that. So there has to be some element of hope, of some unexpected thing. I want to go up on a rooftop and say, 'Hey, listen, all you kids. Listen, all you young lesbians. There is such a rich wonderful sexual experience awaiting you somewhere over the rainbow. You haven't reached it yet.'"

For Dolores, being in this relationship is not simply a wonderful surprise; it's also afforded her the opportunity to do things differently. While she was in the closet in her forties and fifties, being older made her realize she didn't want to live that kind of double life anymore. "I had not come out with any of my children when I was in my other relationship for eighteen years. Then I guess I grew up a little bit, and I decided that this was not the way I wanted to live. I was not going to live as I had done in the past, in the closet. I just couldn't do it. And it was very liberating for me. It was one of the most liberating moments of my life. And I felt that if for some reason my son was not going to be happy with it, this would have made me very sad. But I was going to go forward, and that has everything to do with the fact that I am older."

It turned out that Dolores's son was very supportive, which was a great relief. And though she was initially reluctant to talk to us, having just come out of the closet with her family, that desire to finally be open to the world prompted Dolores to come out not only for this book but also for *Still Doing It,* the documentary film. Watching Dolores and Ellen on a dance floor at a club, grooving to the music and each other, stealing a kiss, lets you know that passion isn't just for kids.

But age and experience have also made Dolores and Ellen

realize that while their lives are intertwined emotionally and sexually, they don't want to live together. Ellen says, "It's a very positive thing for Dolores and myself because in many ways our lifestyles and our tastes in furnishings and our rhythms of when we get up, when we work are very different. And it's nice to be able to share both apartments and enjoy both but not have to live one hundred percent in one of them. We see each other weekends, from Friday night to Sunday night, and usually one or two days more during the week. We speak on the phone at least three, four, or five times a day." But during the week they are also free to pursue their individual passions: Ellen's activism regarding senior issues, especially those affecting gay seniors, and Dolores's participation in the Institute for Retired Professionals and her return to acting.

Dolores and Ellen freely admit that their style and temperament differences might actually have stopped them from getting together when they were younger, when sharing opinions with a lover felt critical, and their different lifestyle choices sometimes cause tensions now. Dolores's kids all have children, and she'd like Ellen to spend more time with her extended family, which Ellen is often unwilling to do. Ellen, on the other hand, who doesn't have grandchildren, likes to spend considerable time with a very dear group of friends (some of whom are ex-lovers) she's known for decades who have become a surrogate family for her, which Dolores is often unwilling to do. How do they handle it? They get irritated. They fight. They separate and spend time with their families and friends. But they come back to a love that gives them the space and autonomy to fully engage in their own busy, expansive lives.

TRUTH OR DARE

S tella (not her real name), seventy-one, is a powerful, attractive woman who goes after what she wants. In the 1980s,
when she became interested in trying out a new career as a life
coach, she applied for a leave of absence from her teaching
job, thinking that if it didn't work out she could always go back.
When they refused her request, Stella took a moment to think,
then realized, "I'd rather be homeless in Grand Central Station
than go back." Instead of winding up destitute, she became
incredibly successful in her new career. In her sixties she com-
pleted her Ph.D. in human and organization systems. Her work
kept her busy and absorbed. A relationship wasn't exactly the
first thing on Stella's mind, but she did miss intimacy.

Then, one New Year's Eve, her friend's husband opened a car
door for her, and when she said she didn't need help he said, "You
don't need a man to do anything for you, do you?" The dare was
too much; within days Stella took a chance and went to a matchmaker, Fay Goldman, of Meaningful Connections. Stella had
gone for it in every other aspect of her life. Here was a chance to
put that energy into her love life. Fay Goldman says that the
reason most older women don't go to matchmakers is because
many won't accept women in their sixties and seventies, and
many women just assume all don't. Luckily for Stella her single-
mindedness led her to someone who could help her. And Stella
made quite an impression on Fay. "With Stella, I remember her
energy level and her aliveness, and she was sorta excited about
life and really just refreshing, very much alive, very interested in

things. You could feel her energy, you know, just very very up, positive energy." Fay quickly thought of a few matches for her.

When Stella met her lover he was only the second man she went out with, but sparks did fly. And she soon discovered that she had an opportunity to be as daring in the bedroom as she had been in her career, to take emotional risks and try out new relationship roles. Stella realized that age and experience and this particular man all liberated her sexually. "I was able to talk about what I wanted, what I didn't want, what I liked. I'm fresher and saucier and more open about sex with him than with anybody [before him]."

It was wonderful to have a lover, and there's no doubt that Stella won the dare, but for a long time she was haunted by the idea that her boyfriend wasn't a perfect match. They were different from each other in a number of respects. He is an academic, Stella a businesswoman. He is very polite, she less formal. He describes Stella as a postmodernist. Compared to Stella he's traditional. Stella very seriously considered breaking off the relationship because of these differences, but after struggling with it for a while, she realized that this was old baggage from her childhood. They didn't live together, so why did they have to be clones? When she thought about it, she saw that in fact this generous, kind man offered her a richer life than she had ever had before. With other lovers in the past who were less consistent she worried a lot about when they might get together. With this man, during the week she could see friends, do her work, go to the gym, knowing that a sexy, intimate weekend awaited her. She'd developed a completely new relationship with her own sexuality, and there was no way she was going to give up that exploration. Now she has let go of the ambivalence and is walking around her apartment naked for the first time, giving blow jobs for the first time, and having the best sex of her life.

When Kate, eighty-two, whose impish smile gives her a youthful quality despite a deeply lined face, met her boyfriend, David (eight years her junior) on a walk in her San Francisco neighborhood, her kids were a little worried. "My kids were just in wonder about this guy . . . who he was and why he moved into my house. That was eight years ago. Now they are fine. I guess they were protective of their dear little mother." But today, "David continues to do his own thing. He hikes and does volunteer work for a writers' group and I am teaching one class in infant-toddler development. I am also a City Guide, give walks in the neighborhood once a month, and I continue with Children at the Arboretum. Not bad for almost eighty-three." Kate feels blessed after living through her husband's long bout with multiple sclerosis and ultimate passing to have a relationship with a man who'd like to have sex once or twice a night. She revels in the fact that at this point in her life she can live with someone without getting married, and have her own finances, her own social life, which is what she thinks she would have wanted when she was younger, had it been socially acceptable at the time.

Contrary to stereotypes of older people as needy and dependent, the women we interviewed all clearly value their independence. In fact we were surprised to find out how many women like Stella, Dolores, and Ellen love but don't want to live with their partners. Many said their youthful romantic image of love and sex was all about merging, finding someone they could totally identify with, but they often lost a part of themselves in the process. Over and over again they told us that a great thing about being older was being able to love without losing yourself or your identity. As matchmaker Fay Goldman points out, one of the perks of getting older is being able to be with someone who is different, and that, in and of itself, fosters a greater sense of autonomy and self. That space, whether it's created by living separately or being more independent, can also help keep one's sex life truly fresh.

While it wasn't hard to find couples to interview who had met in later life, finding long-term couples proved more difficult. We searched for years and found only a few women in very long-term relationships who were willing to be interviewed. Many refused without offering explanation. Others told us they weren't comfortable revealing their partner's intimate lives. It's also possible that their unwillingness to talk is a reflection of how hard it is to maintain vibrant sexual relationships over time. But Evelyn (not her real name) and futurist Maddie Dychtwald, who predicts trends, prove that long-term sexual relationships definitely exist and can maintain their energy.

Evelyn, sixty, an African-American woman with the quiet, strong, self-possessed energy of a dancer, married a white man in 1968 at the height of the civil rights movement. Many people viewed it as a radical act. Evelyn's parents were dead set against the marriage, particularly because of her husband's radical politics. At one point he was jailed for political action in Berkeley. They met at college, but almost immediately were separated when Evelyn went abroad for a year to study.

Remarkably, Evelyn and her husband turned both the racial and geographic challenges to their advantage. They worked against the distance by making communication a priority, sending letters and writing poetry to each other, which allowed them to get to know each other in a profound way. Evelyn describes the letters as "part of the sealing of our marriage." The way that her husband faced challenges made him even more attractive to Evelyn: "There was something about him being both funny and a risk taker and just an extremely lively individual that I found very, very engaging. We were very much in love when we started." Their activism led them to travel, and they lived for five years in Africa, where the fact that they were a mixed-race couple didn't seem to raise eyebrows and they could live their lives together more easily, "away from the glare of the civil rights movement and people challenging a black/white couple." All that was thirty years ago. Since then, they've had two children, moved from New York to Washington, D.C., and endured the fear caused by Evelyn's husband's heart attack thirteen years ago.

After all this time, when Evelyn talks about her husband, it's clear the heat is still there. In fact, their sexual connection has been heightened by the fact that they no longer have to attend to their children's daily needs. Evelyn still giggles on the phone when she describes how sexy her husband is. But despite the obvious chemistry, they work on it. They respect each other's space, and they know that if they have periods of distance the passion will come back. From the beginning their relationship has been based on sexual chemistry and a deep commitment to working out problems.

While Evelyn's husband was an academic superstar right out of the gate, Evelyn calls herself a late bloomer. After a career as a dancer, then as a family therapist, she went back to school again and just got a new job at a community learning center. Her career upswing is happening just at a point when her husband's career has faced some decline. Though she acknowledges that he's in a long-term depression, she refuses to devote her life to pulling him out of it. "For me, I can certainly understand where the impetus for wanting to change someone would come from, but if they're going to be responsible, active agents in their lives then they've got to want to change. I think that's really the bottom line. I know my husband is frustrated with how he perceives the world right now, but he could also have a very different take on it. I know his take on it is 'This is frustrating. I'm a failure. I wish there was a way to change this end of my life.' And I can't change that for him." While Evelyn clearly cares deeply for her husband she knows she can't fix his life for him. Instead she focuses both on her own life, which is so exciting to her right now, and on enjoying the things that really bring her husband and her close to each other, including a home they just bought in Mexico and their strong physical attraction to each other.

"If I look back at it now I can see a point where people would say, 'Boy, this marriage isn't going to last.' My husband is a very intellectual person, a very academic person, a very bookish person also. But I think we've grown to be much more alike in ways that have helped to sustain the marriage: love of nature, love of being outdoors, love of biking, love of traveling together, and love for raising this family together has really been a lifetime's work. I think even over the many twists and turns in the relationship I don't think there's ever been a time where either one of us felt like 'I'm throwing in the towel. I'm packing it in.' We've been really committed to each other over these thirty-six years." And despite the fact that her husband has faced some hard times of late, that commitment on Evelyn's part isn't going anywhere.

THE "HONEYMOON"

Perhaps the illusion those of us not lucky enough to have found an enduring long-term relationship have is that it "just happens." Maddie's twenty-five-year marriage continues to be vital because of constant work and communication. She and her husband, eminent futurist Ken Dychtwald, two vibrant, extremely attractive individuals, go away for a week every year. During the trip they are remarried in a different place by a different religious institution. It sounds like a honeymoon, but Maddie thinks of it as the "survival kit for marriage."

Throughout this annual week they check in with each other about what they have been doing well with each other, what needs to be changed, and what they need to improve. According to Maddie, "The process of doing that together is what gives our relationship longevity. It causes reinvention. It's like editing a book: You want to put in all the good and take out all the bad." It's a way of celebrating their partnership together and celebrating changes in their lives. When we asked Maddie if things ever come up during this week together that they have been completely oblivious to, she said no. But as she went on to point out, there's a major difference between recognizing that there's a problem and having the time to really address the issue.

Their relationship gives them the support to do their own thing, but they never take it for granted. Each is responsible for bringing new life to the relationship. Maddie says, "I think reinvention is the key, the idea that you don't have to be who you were when you were younger. You can really figure out the new you." Maddie and her husband are two vital, turned-on people who are willing to do what it takes to keep the connection between them alive—sexually and otherwise.

Even while Maddie recognizes that her relationship with Ken has been immensely successful and fulfilling, she regards her relationship as unique. She explains, "I don't think everybody's marriage is going to be long. There's a quote by Margaret Mead: 'I've been married three times, all successful.' And I think there's some truth to that. Some people will have more than one long-term monogamous relationship that fits the needs of their life at that point, while others will use methods to make their marriages change as they change, and then other people will choose to be married at some points and at other points be single. I think that options will be really out there and open and more flexible. That's the key: You choose the lifestyle that you want. You choose not to be dictated to just because you're a certain age. You know, just because you're sixty-five doesn't mean that you want to retire, that you're old, that you want to stop being open to fresh ideas and new experiences."

LEAVING MARRIAGES

The truth is that many people don't have such great relationships, and while more men do leave their marriages than women, there is a growing number of older women not willing to stay in marriages that are safe but no longer alive. Elli, seventy-one, a singer and actress whose career is just taking off, Elizabeth, seventy-four, a former housewife and mother, and Shelley, sixty-six, who is the head of a local branch of the

National Employment Lawyers Association, three sexy older women, had to face the fact that after years of trying, their marriages weren't working. They had to choose between staying in a relationship that was unfulfilling or daring to get out and look for a more dynamic life. Elizabeth says, "I was married for thirty-four years. My husband was pretty domineering, and I was pretty easygoing. I didn't know how to speak up for my own rights. He didn't abuse me, but verbally he was difficult at times. And that's a kind of abuse, I know. But I went to therapy and tried to make the marriage better, but he wouldn't go. So in therapy I was able to get up enough strength and nerve to make the break, and I've never regretted it. I've really had a good fifteen years [since I left him]." Elizabeth told us, "The worst part was telling people that I was getting a divorce. It was still sort of a stigma. So that was probably the worst part. But once I got over that and dealt with my children, they were pretty good about it. I have a son, fifty, a daughter, forty-eight, and another daughter, forty-two. So they were all grown and married when I got a divorce. So, like I said, once I decided to do it, I never looked back, never regretted it."

Elli tells how long the decision to leave her husband weighed on her before she made up her mind. She had to face the fear of being alone at fifty-seven and not being able to find someone new. But "there were fifteen years where I'd given up my creative goals, where I wasn't happy, and then the next year I asked my husband to leave, which was a very big deal. I'd been on the fence for sixteen years." Being single again "was a huge choice and change in my life." But she told herself, "You've got to end this relationship; it's way overdue." She used her next birthday as the deadline, telling her husband he had to leave by then. "So for my fifty-eighth birthday my husband finally left. When I finally did it I couldn't help feeling, You're fifty-eight! Who's going to want you?"

But almost immediately, the gift of her creative energy started to come back to her. After feeling mute and drained, she started singing and acting again. She felt wonderful. Her friends and neighbors all noticed how much younger and happier she looked. People would come up to her and say, "You look great. What's going on?" She tells how after hearing that she had broken up with her husband, some people were excited for her but others thought she was crazy. Some people "were horrified, and they never spoke to me again because it was so threatening. Not even knowing my age, just the idea that I had the balls to break up with a man, when everyone's running around the city, going, 'Where are they?' "

Elli soon met a man she was with for the next eight years. But this doesn't happen for all women—not by a long shot. There is a huge partner gap, and the truth is that not every older woman who leaves her husband is going to find a man her age to be with.

According to the New York Times, *there has been a sharp increase in the number of divorces by people sixty-five and older ("The 37-Year Itch," August 8, 2004). As sixty-five-year-old New York matrimonial lawyer Robert Stephen Cohen comments, "You're looking at seventeen, eighteen years of living. And that's a long time. And those years could be especially vibrant if you can have a vibrant sex life. The golden pond is now at ninety, not seventy."*

STATISTICS

- In 1960, only 1.6 percent of older men and 1.5 percent of women age sixty-five and older were divorced, but, by 2003, 7 percent of older men and 8.6 percent of older women were divorced and had not remarried. The trend may be continuing. In 2003, among people in their early sixties 12.2 percent of men and 15.9 percent of women were divorced.[1]

- In 2003, older men were more likely than older women to be married (71 percent vs. 41 percent). Three quarters (74 percent) of men age sixty-five to seventy-four were married, compared to roughly half (54 percent) of women in the same age group. The proportion married was lower at older ages: 34 percent of women age seventy-five to eighty-four and 13 percent of women eighty-five and older. Among their male counterparts, the proportions were higher: 70 percent of men age seventy-five to eighty-four were married, and even among men age eighty-five and older, the majority were married (56 percent).[2]

3.

THE PARTNER GAP

Dating and mating is a gamble at any age, but later in life the deck is stacked a little differently for women.

The number of people alive today who are over sixty is growing exponentially, but since women have a propensity to live longer than their male counterparts, the partner gap between men and women is widening along with it. By the age of sixty-five, there are thirty-three single men for every one hundred single women.[3] Then, skewing the numbers even more, older men tend to date younger women, while older women more often stick to men in their own age group.[4] There simply aren't enough older men for older women, leaving many without potential partners, particularly those who aren't open to alternative relationships.

- Seventy-one percent of men over the age of sixty-five are married, as compared with only 41 percent of women.
- Almost half (47.6 percent) of women seventy-five and older live alone.
- Over half the women in America are widowed. There are three times as many widows as widowers.
- Widowhood is more common among older women than older men. Women sixty-five and older were three times as likely as men of the same age to be widowed: 44 percent versus 14 percent. The proportion widowed is higher at older ages and higher for women than for men. In 2003, 78 percent of women age eighty-five and over were widowed, compared to 35 percent of men.[5]

Statistics taken from U.S. Census Bureau, Current Population Reports, 65+ in the United States: 2005.

FIRST CHALLENGE: NOT ENOUGH
MEN TO GO AROUND

For Freddie, seventy-nine, still a working therapist, the death of her husband meant the loss of the vibrant sex life they had shared. She was totally unprepared. "From the time I was nineteen until after Sidney died [when I was fifty-five], sex was extremely important to me. One of the first thoughts I had after he died was, Well, I wonder if I will ever have sex again. And then I dropped that thought. After a number of years I tried to see if there were any [available] men around, but there was a feeling of if I want to do anything at all, I was going to be the one doing the pursuing. I'm not saying women shouldn't pursue men, but I wasn't very good at it. I found that there were very few in my age range, that the only way to arrange [meeting a single man] is to find somebody whose wife has just died and pounce on him. I met widowers whose wives had died only months ago, and they were already in new relationships. And the ones that didn't [get involved with another woman rather quickly] were men who seemed too hurt by their loss to want to ever get into another relationship."

For the first time in her life, Freddie began to lose touch with her sexuality. She felt herself trying to put the brakes on her sex drive. "I suppressed all my sexual feelings. I tried not to think about it. I tried not to feel them unless they sneaked up on me. Sometimes when it's been months and I haven't felt anything and then suddenly something comes up and I begin to have very strong feelings, then I guess I'm surprised that they're still that strong."

SECOND CHALLENGE: OLDER MEN OFTEN WANT YOUNGER WOMEN

What really clinched Freddie's frustration was that of the few single older men she did meet, most were looking for younger women. "It was as if nobody really looked at me anymore. I felt invisible."

Shelley, sixty-six, had the same kind of "rude awakening" when she decided to divorce her husband in her late fifties. As she tried to date her male contemporaries, she learned that while their bodies might have aged, their taste in women hadn't. She says, "I've always felt like a sexual being, and then when I became single and wound up being in this world of singledom I thought, Hey, this is going to be fun. This is gonna be great. Didn't happen!"

For Shelley, an unusually attractive, confident woman, the situation was hard to swallow. Her confidence and sex drive had helped her decide to divorce her husband in the first place to find a more fulfilling relationship. Her majestic good looks should have instantly grabbed the attention of many men, but instead she felt she wasn't even registering on most men's radar. "I really thought that my persona hadn't changed over all these years, that I was still Shelley and this sexual being and attractive to men. It's been a little frustrating and a little depressing, because I still feel that I'm a vital sexual human being and I'm not able to express it."

Shelley wanted to pursue men, but it was hard to translate her intentions into real action. "I [had] fantasies that I could just have these isolated one-nighters, but I could not be the aggressor, which was very interesting to me because I'm a rather assertive, aggressive person. And I found myself being very reticent when it came to men. I couldn't make eye contact. I'm not sure what that was all about. I think it was probably because I was in a thirty-year marriage and I hadn't been with anyone [else] in all those years." Shelley felt like she was being disqualified from the dating game merely because of her age.

On the other hand, Joani, seventy, decided to really push it. As a sex expert who started the legendary Good Vibrations sex shop in San Francisco in the 1970s, she has always placed great importance on her sexuality. So she was willing to go out on a limb for it. When it seemed obvious to her that men were looking for younger women, she decided to give them what they were looking for: She created Internet dating profiles and lied about her age. "I listed my age as fifty-five or fifty-six since I noticed that most of the men in their late fifties and sixties were typically searching for women quite a bit younger than themselves, and I wanted to be sure my profile at least showed up in their searches."

Joani lied about her age to draw more men's attention. This isn't to say that she's ever felt complacent about the underlying prejudice at work. She just has a different tactic for reacting to ageism. She says, "We live in a youth culture. We have no respect for the wisdom of our elders. Our culture does not support old people." That's one of the reasons that Joani has decided to live in a co-housing community shared by both younger and older people. But manipulating the rules in the ageist dating game is part of Joani's attempt to undermine the superficial assumptions people make about each other based on their age. After many failed attempts to meet a man on the Internet, Joani did meet someone through the Web with whom she had great sex for over a year. Soon after, she met another man at a workshop with whom she has been involved in a nonmonagamous relationship for a few years.

Fay Goldman, the matchmaker at Meaningful Connections, says that while she doesn't have a plentiful pool, like, for someone in their thirties, she's been surprised at "what I do come up with for women in their sixties." She says that the good news is that more men are opening up to being with women their own age or older, especially men who have been married or had some therapy—the ones she calls more "evolved"—but these guys are still the exception, not the norm.

For many older women, like Freddie, who aren't comfortable going to a matchmaker or going through the inevitable work and disappointment that come with online dating, the partner gap can make the possibility of future romance feel hopeless. Freddie says, "It's almost like a dream: You remember you had it; you remember it was good when you had it; but I'm not going to sit at home and constantly think about it and regret not having it."

THIRD CHALLENGE: MARRIED MEN

Shelley spent five years wondering how to turn her fantasies into reality, but eventually she found a chance to play the extroverted role she had always imagined for herself. One night at dinner with some friends, she started to sense that one of the men at the table was interested in her. It was the sort of opportunity that she had been hoping for, except that she had been looking for an interesting eligible bachelor, not a married man. It wasn't a perfect situation, but Shelley couldn't tune out the attention she was getting from him. She remembers feeling herself come alive sexually. "The restaurant we were in played music. Nobody was dancing because there was no dance floor, and he asked me to dance. Now this is a man who was unavailable, as I said, and then something happened to me. I felt a great attraction, and I think it was probably because he was really coming on to me and feeling very sexually attracted to me. So I responded, not consciously, of course, and then that felt really good. And later on, we did go to a place where there was dancing, and I [laughs] I became very extroverted, open, and I'm dancing on the dance floor like I was dancing for him. And he wasn't dancing anymore. He kind of stepped back, and of course I had had one or two drinks but that generally doesn't affect me too much, and I just felt the whole thing pouring out of me, all of the pent-up sexuality that I had and this yearning that I had, I felt it all pour out of me, and it was great. I felt totally free."

When he called her later in the week, she was even bolder. He sounded awkward and shy during the conversation, but they made tentative plans to see a jazz combo that evening. But after Shelley hung up with him she thought, I don't want to go hear a jazz combo with him, I want to bring him back to my apartment. She called him back right away and revised the plan, telling him, "I've rethought the evening. Would you like to come to my apartment and I'll have dinner for you?" This time, when they hung up the phone with each other, the plans were certain. "I think that was an offer he couldn't refuse, and he came to my apartment and of course I wasn't cooking. I had other things in mind, and suffice it to say we never had dinner that night."

The relationship was monumental for Shelley, because it was her first big relationship after ending her marriage. It gave her the chance to explore her sexuality with someone new. The night he came over for "dinner," Shelley remembers how he assured her, "I'm not here purely for sex." She instantly responded, "Well, you may not be, but I am." For Shelley, their sex was the key. "The evening evolved, and it was wonderful, it was great, it was freeing, and he was an incredible lover. But oh, taking off my clothes, the thought of taking off my clothes. I was conscious of it; I thought about that, and I said, 'Oh my God, you know, my body doesn't look like it did before in my youth, and I much prefer myself clothed rather than undressed." But when the time came, I was fine with it. I mean, I had very low lighting and candles, and, you know, we all look very well under candlelight, but I really didn't think about it and I just did it. It was a natural thing. I wanted to do it, and I did. And he certainly wasn't a beauty, you know. I think you kind of get over that because what is the point, you know; we're all not beautiful and youthful forever, and to kind of hold back and deprive yourself of something because of how you think you look, the vanity part of it, you're missing out."

And after five years of not having sex, Shelley truly enjoyed this man's lovemaking. "I'm talking hours, and not that he was able to sustain an erection, mind you, but he just knew how to make me feel wonderful. Just touching and caressing, all nurturing, and I asked him if he learned how to satisfy a woman from being with so many over the years, and he said he did. Which is in his favor and to his credit. So, I mean, I can't even tell you specifically. It was nothing outrageous; it was the way he made me feel and the way I got excited in the relationship, in the intimacy of the sex."

The fact that he was married, that their meetings were secretive was all tangential at the beginning. Shelley was able to express herself again "as a vital sexual human being," but ultimately it became too painful. "I was out of my marriage five years and I had not had the experience of being with a man and I just let myself get a little carried away, and I really knew in my heart of hearts that it was never gonna evolve into anything more than it was and I would be hurt constantly if I tried to reach him on the phone and had to play cat and mouse. I don't need that shit. That's not for me." So she eventually ended the relationship.

Joani, on the other hand, has no issues about sleeping with men who have commitments to other women. As a polyamorist, she isn't looking for monogamy, but she is looking for relationships based on trust and openness and honesty, which she doesn't always find. She told us, "Last month I was sitting in the airport reading *The Ethical Slut: A Bible for Polyamorists,* and a seventy-four-year-old guy came over to me and started talking to me about the book. I had breakfast with him a couple of weeks later. Although I find [him] quite interesting and reasonably attractive I'm not interested in pursuing even a friendship with him because he has let me know that his wife would be very uncomfortable with that . . . and he'd never tell her that he'd even met me.

"Though I'm open to becoming intimate with a man who is in a committed relationship with someone else—assuming his partner is truly okay with him being with me—I'm not willing to just fill in an empty spot in his sex life or, for that matter, any other part of his life." We asked Joani what appealed to her about an open relationship, and she told us, "My main reason for wanting an open relationship is because I think there's plenty of love to go around and that we all deserve to get as much of it as we can in our all-too-short lives."

Clearly women of all ages have different needs. The affair that worked for Shelley for a while would never interest Joani. And, certainly, the open relationships that Joani finds ideal would be too much for many people to handle.

FOURTH CHALLENGE: RELATIONSHIPS WITH OLDER MEN ARE OFTEN SHORT (BUT SWEET)

Even when women do find men their age, their relationships are often short-lived. After years of being alone, Elaine, eighty, met a new lover. "A very nice man whom I've known for

years. He was divorced and my age, also African American. It
was wonderful! I knew him through my senior center. In a small
town like this, most all of us know each other. I knew his wife. He
had two sons by that marriage, and I knew one of them very well
because he worked at our local hospital. He just approached me,
saying, 'You know, I'm just so tired of eating alone. Would you
consider going out for dinner some evening with me?' And I said,
'Of course!' And it just kind of worked its way into a relationship. And we did things like go to Atlantic City for the weekend,
eat at the nicest restaurants. He drove, so we did a lot of sightsee-
ing. I saw parts of Rhode Island that . . .I had [never] seen. And,
you know, I loved it. I loved it. It was a sexual relationship to an
extent. We did a lot of petting. We tried intercourse, and it worked
well for us. We always used to laugh, and I would tell him, 'I'm
gonna write a book: *Sex After Seventy: We Do It Our Way.*' And
we'd laugh about that. I dated him for a little over two years. But
then he died. Thanksgiving Day it will be exactly two years."

Elaine is alone again, but she's living a full life, doing volunteer work, traveling with family and friends. Perhaps having lived
through cancer herself and having seen some of her close friends
die from it, she wasn't as shocked by her partner's death as someone younger would have been. In any event, Elaine accepted the
loss with grace. While she remembers her partner fondly, her
focus is on the here and now, and that includes still being open to
meeting another partner.

Penny, eighty-five, and in a new romance, married at twenty-
two. Despite the fact that her husband was not the most attentive
lover, she had just celebrated her fiftieth-wedding anniversary
on a cruise when he died from a heart attack. A year later, at
seventy-three, she met another man in Florida, where she and

her husband had moved after years of living in Indiana. "He filled a gap that I didn't have with my first husband. My first husband was very loving, but he was a little on the cold side. He was not amorous. He didn't come up and give me a hug. [My new love] might pat me on the fanny or give me a loving touch or lean over and kiss me if he felt like it, whereas my first husband would never dream of doing that. [My first husband] was very private with his concern and admiration of me. He just held it off. When I got together with my new lover, I thought I had died and gone to heaven." Penny and her new love had a whirlwind romance, quickly married, and traveled around the world. But fourteen months later he, too, died of cancer. "We had one Christmas together. We didn't have quite a year of full-fledged living, but we had a wonderful honeymoon in England and Russia. The first Christmas we had we took another cruise down to the Caribbean. He was still very amorous."

Despite being devastated Penny met another man a year later whom she dated for a number of years. And at eighty-four, after moving into a retirement community in Florida and struggling through a depression caused by this life change, she got involved with yet another man with whom she is currently passionately involved. Her new boyfriend, a former New Yorker, called after spotting her and asked her out to dinner. She said, not wanting to seem too eager, "I'll have to check my book." But she was very excited. A year later they eat together every day, go touring in her sports car, and enjoy the delights of sex. For Penny the trick now is loving with the knowledge that impermanence is a part of life and having fun is the only defense.

Ruth, who met her husband, Harry, at sixty-four after thirty years of being single, is clearly affected both by her knowledge that men tend to die earlier than women and by the reality of the partner gap. She savors their relationship but remains philosophical about the likelihood that she might grow old alone. "One of the things about having Harry in my life is, I guess, I'm a little afraid to let myself fall into that reverie or thought that it's wonderful to have someone to grow old with. Either I think it might change, or I don't want to have regrets. So, I guess my sense is, well, if Harry is not here at some point and I have to grow old alone I don't want to yearn for the time when I had him. I don't think that I think of my husband as someone who's going to take care of me if something happens. All I can think about now is the nice part of having someone with me in these years and not having to go at it by myself all the time, and that is very nice. It's very special, and I feel very lucky that I met and have him now."

The fact that time spent with a lover may very well be fleeting makes relationships between older people poignant. Many of the women that we spoke with told us that as they age they have learned to develop the ability to fully give of themselves sexually and emotionally while maintaining a more autonomous sense of their lives as a whole. Their ability to resurrect their lives, their spirit, and their thirst for new connection even in the face of the death of partners demonstrates the phenomenal resilience of the human spirit.

FEMALE BONDING

One of the results of the partner gap is that if you go into any major city or most small towns, for that matter, you will find tightly knit groups of single older women (divorcees, widows, and women who have always been single) who socialize and take care of one another. Freddie says, "Well, I think that women are important to each other at all stages of life. Because they, in a way, understand life in a way that is very different from the way men do. And I'm not talking about men that are not good to their wives or not good husbands or good fathers. I don't think men see life in quite the same way. I think that women become even more important to each other as they get older since they outlive men. And women who are alone don't tend to have as many contacts with other couples as they did when they were married. So I really appreciate my friends at this point in my life. A few of my very oldest friends have died, and that's very hard. But the friends I have that are still here, we do things together, we go out to dinner, to the theater, hear music, go to parties. We also check in on each other, run errands if someone's sick. Sometimes in the bigger world I feel invisible, but with my friends I feel very vital."

Shelley took community with women to the next level and bought a house at the beach with her friend Susan that she never could have afforded on her own. "It's worked out really well. I love going there. Even if I only go for a day and a half, it's revitalizing. As soon as I hit a certain point driving to it, I feel my whole body go into this wonderful, relaxed mode." She and her housemate have worked it out so they're there together and alone, getting the best of both. " I love being there by myself when I'm by myself. Susan comes out Thursday to Monday, so I basically have Tuesday and Wednesday there alone, and I do like that time by myself. But we do things together all the time when she's here."

One thing Shelley finds she often has to contend with is that people don't always recognize their connection as housemates. "I mean, it's not an issue really, but I know more people out there because I do group things, and she does none of that. I play tennis, I spin, so I meet many more people. So on occasion I've been invited for dinner and I've had to say, you know, I have a housemate. And it kind of pisses me off . . . people sort of know that I have a housemate, but don't they understand that [not inviting her] is not nice? If it were a man living with me, would they not include him? If I wasn't married but had a significant other in my house, would they not include him? Anyway. So we do a lot of things together. And we share many interests . . . very similar interests. . . . It's absolutely nice. I would never want to be there alone all the time." Shelley told us she thinks she'll ultimately sell the house. "It's a lot of work." But for now Susan and Shelley have joined forces to realize a dream.

With the number of women living without partners now reaching over 51 percent, we're going to see more and more nonromantic cohabitants like Susan and Shelley. As more women realize they may never get married again, or even for the first time, women will surely get into partnerships with other women, whether it's to buy a house together or to travel around the world.

KEEPING THE HOPE ALIVE

While having female friends is clearly crucial, for many older women it's hard to keep the hope of becoming involved with a man alive in the face of how hard it is to meet one, but that doesn't mean sexual thoughts and feelings don't creep in. Shelley says, "Sometimes when I'm in a room with men, I have fantasies that they're all thinking, fantasizing about me, like going to bed with me and what would it be like. There are periods of time that I think about it, and I don't even miss it. And then there are times that . . . I think about it a lot, you know, feeling sexual, wanting to be sexual. I think I think about it more than I don't think about it. I know I think about it when I walk down the street, I even observe if men are looking at me and [I wonder if I am] still that attractive, sexual being. And even though in my heart I feel I'm a feminist, you know, it's still a very natural man/ woman kind of thing when I see men looking at me on the street. I don't mean like construction workers doing their number, but even that probably would be flattering. But it's nice to know that you're still viewed as someone with appeal." Yet, despite being a stunning, healthy woman, Shelley is not in any way actively seeking a romantic partner.

Joani, on the other hand, sees the search and admittance to wanting partners and sex as part of being fully alive. A polyamorist, she is open to a new lover even when she has one, and now with her current relationship ending, she very much wants to connect with someone new. Joani's had her profile on Internet dating services for years.

When you go to *Joani6* on the very popular *match.com* online service, you're greeted by a warm, attractive woman on a country road. The slightly diffused earth tones behind her are mirrored by an earthy woman, clearly sexy and full of life. Her salt-and-pepper hair and wrinkles give depth to her smile. She's not young, but she's totally sexy. The headline of her profile reads: "In these uncertain times, I will remain open to the miracle that is each moment." In opposition to most people, who list all that they are, she lists all that she is not: not conservative, not afraid of sex, not tall.

And Joani has finally decided to be more honest about her age.

She writes, "You may have seen me on here before or on Green Singles, where up until now I've not told the truth about my age in the matching part, because I thought if I did, I'd not show up in the searches of men around my age. It's time to come clean, however. I'm still not going to give you my exact age, but I will tell you that I'm over sixty-five. And in case you are wondering, yes, my pictures are recent."

MEETING THE CHALLENGES, CHANGING THE GAME

Whether Joani's search will continue to provide her with more men her own age is unclear. Certainly her willingness to be in alternative situations increases her odds. While women like Freddie told us they would like to be open to sexual experimentation, she says, "For women of my generation that may be more difficult." She predicts, however, that we are on the cusp of big changes. "I think that in the future as women continue to outlive men, women will be more and more open to exploring different kinds of sexuality."

Sexual researchers Starr and Weiner confirm Freddie's prediction: "The [generation of women

In 1900 the life expectancy for white women in the United States was only 48.7 and for African-American women 33.5. The latest report of the Centers for Disease Control reports that the average life expectancy in the United States is now 80.5 for white women and 76.1 for African-American women.

- *In the last one hundred years the life expectancy of women has increased by more than thirty years.*

who will be older in 2010] will have fewer hesitations about exploring whatever workable lifestyles are available. They will not sit back and accept their lot, abandoning their sexuality. They will explore whatever lifestyle options are open to them," bringing the don't-knock-it-'til-you-try-it spirit of the '60s and '70s into their later years. Ken Dychtwald, noted futurist and author of *Age Wave and Age Power,* says, "As a society we will have to become more accepting [of older women's] relationships with younger men, homosexuality, and share-a-man relationships."

Life expectancy, especially for women, is longer than ever before in human history. As we age we're going to have the chance to live fuller lives, to explore totally new aspects of ourselves. As the baby-boomer generation starts to discover the kind of lives they want later in life, they will be setting the trend for all of us.

While this phenomenon is about to explode, there are already women in their seventies and eighties living wild lives.

4.

OLDER AND WILDER:
NONTRADITIONAL RELATIONSHIPS

Few people realize just how many women there are in their sixties, seventies, and eighties today who are enjoying alternative relationships. Despite having been born in much more conservative times, they choose lifestyles that make many younger women look tame by comparison. Rather than resign themselves to a sexless future, they are shocking their children and grandchildren by getting together with younger (sometimes much younger!) men, dating more than one man at a time, making share-a-man arrangements, or hooking up with another woman for the first time. Older age means less time left on this earth. For some women this knowledge inspires a willingness to take risks and open new doors of possibility.

A YOUNGER MAN

Ever since the 1960s, when Betty, now seventy-eight, left an unhappy marriage and found herself right smack in the middle of the sexual revolution, she's been experimenting with the playful and liberating possibilities of sex. Much of her work has been dedicated to running masturbation workshops to help women better know, explore, and enjoy their bodies. So it was clear she would do whatever it took to keep sex a high priority. But even Betty was caught off guard by the direction her sex life took in her late sixties.

As a "committed single," always open to new sexual adventures, she started to use Internet chat rooms as a playground for her fantasies, and in the process met Erik, now thirty-one. "For a period, I don't know, it was three or four, five months he was sending me these e-mails, and I would send ones back and say that was wonderful, I love it, send me another one, and then one day I wrote: If you're ever in the New York area come and see me. It was fun to have the fantasy. I really never expected it to happen. He eventually came to New York, and I thought, I've done a stupid thing. I'm going to lose my fantasy. So I open up the apartment door and in walks this six-foot-tall, gorgeous man with a pencil mustache and a goatee. He had a long coat with a red shirt and a tie. He was beautiful. And there was no doubt in my mind, Oh, I want to fuck this kid. The energy was right there instantly." Instead of destroying her fantasy, Erik brought it to life.

But being with a much younger man wasn't without challenges, even for Betty, who is extremely comfortable with her sexuality. "When he came in I thought, Oh, God, I'm going to have to take off my clothes, and here I am with this beautiful young body and I'm an aging body. And I thought, Betty move through it. . . . And I have continued to move through it, and I will continue to move through it." Erik adds, "We met when she was sixty-nine and I was [twenty-two and] I was amazed at how good she looked at sixty-nine, but I remember when she first got nude she obviously didn't have a body that was the same as [that of] a younger woman. So there was a part of me that got uneasy, but the other part of me said what you're going to be gaining is a lot more powerful than petty concerns of appearance." He stops and thinks a moment. "But if Betty had been more consistently uncomfortable with her body image, then I think eventually it would start to wear. I think I would get tired of hearing it."

Betty chimes in. "But it's always there. That challenge is always there. Women all have self-image, body-image [issues]. . . . I fight with it all the time. I don't think it ever goes away. But if we're going to live in a world that is strictly 'you can only have sex if you're young and beautiful' it's pathetic."

Age difference aside, their personalities were compatible and the sex incredible. Betty says, "We were having way more sex than I thought was possible for a woman my age," and Erik quickly decided that he wanted to move in with her, to be her lover as well as to work with her and become a sex educator himself. Betty was amazed and slightly skeptical. "I never intended having a partner at this late stage. And if I did have a partner I assumed it would be a woman. Because what I saw [was] that the guys that interested me were all taking younger women." When Betty met Erik she initially thought it would just be a quick

affair, but when he pushed to come live with her it was an opportunity she just couldn't refuse.

But many people found it hard to swallow. People noticed
them and made comments wherever they went. "My favorite one
was when we went into a restaurant and this woman was eyeball-
ing us and I heard her turn to the guy she was with and she said,
'Good God! That woman is twenty years older than him.' And
we sat down and I said, 'I think I should go over and thank her
because actually I'm forty years older. Yes, a lot of people think
it's disgusting that I have a young lover. I don't give a rat's ass."

Even some of their friends and family were uncomfortable
with a relationship that clearly breaks all social taboos. Erik's best
friend was awkward around Betty. "The first few times Matt
came over, he couldn't even make eye contact with me. I'm sure
he couldn't cope with the concept of Erik being with a woman
who was so much older. So I would just do my own thing, and
they'd do their own thing. It took almost a year before he warmed
up. And now we're buddies."

Erik's extended family was also resistant to the relationship.
His mother accepted it because she liked Betty so much, but Erik
and Betty had been living together for seven years before they
were invited to any of Erik's extended-family events. Betty says,
"We recently were invited out to Pelham, this very fancy neighborhood, because he has cousins out there [who] are successful.
And Erik has been living here with me, we're in our seventh year
now, and we never heard from them. And one day they call up and
say, Oh, this one's in town and that one's in town, why don't you
come out? And I didn't want to go, but then I thought, This is
my chance to meet the Wilkinson clan, so we did. And within
moments [of arriving I see] the big papa cat. We're walking towards

each other, you know: big smile, 'hi,' shake hands. And [Big Papa Cat] looked over and he said, 'I think we're contemporaries.' And I said, 'I'm seventy-six. How old are you?' Boom. Right at it. And he said, 'Seventy-seven.' I said, 'Yup, I'll be seventy-seven in August. So we're contemporaries, all right.' And then we get in the car—and I love to stick it toe to toe with power dudes. It's one of my favorite things. So he's really, he's so full of himself, he's, you know, doing his résumé, so to speak, and he picks up his latest documentary. (He does documentaries for *National Geographic*.) So he hands me his latest DVD. And I do not know why, but when we left the house, I put my DVD, my new one, in my purse. And I never carry a purse. There was some instinct. So, he hands me his, and I reach in and I hand him mine, *Orgasmic Women*. And so he set it down inside. And when I was getting out of the car, I said, 'You better turn that over or someone will break into your car if they see it, because they'll think it's porn. Yeah, you might think it's porn, [too,] but let me know what you think.'

"So then we meet at the restaurant, and here comes his wife, who's also my contemporary. Her body looked ravaged and she was walking with a cane, and she seemed so unhappy. So we sit down, and we start having lunch. And I banter. He does his thing, and I'm right there. Because he's, like, you know, everybody just sits at his feet. So I'm in there with him, doing the dance. And early on I said, 'Well, you know, Erik is going to be a fabulous sex educator because he's learning a lot. And we're really focused on teaching sexual skills, and most people don't even think there is such a thing because you guys think you know everything that you need to know about female sexuality, but if you really ask any woman'—and I looked over at Jean, his wife—'she will tell you that you don't know shit.' And she said, 'You've got that right.' I mean, boy, I made a connection, and she was on my side from that moment on. I mean, I really bonded at that point with her. So that was fun."

Betty's irreverent humor comes from the fact that she doesn't care what other people think about her. She attributes her zesty quality to her mother and what a straight shooter she was. "My mom never minced words, and I will eternally be grateful for that model." Whatever the origins, Betty is clearly confident that she will be okay with whatever happens next. She loves having Erik in her life but is also aware that life changes and that at any point he might want a different situation. "I think it's so great that at my age I'm having this fabulous relationship with this beautiful young man. Am I going to stay with him? Who knows? And I've said this to him: Don't ever feel that you are obligated to stay with me. For me it's always the adventure. I'm looking for the next adventure, and I think that's what creativity is about."

Tamara, sixty-nine, the stylish graphic artist we met in a doctor's office, is also having a relationship with a man much younger than she. Twenty-five years younger, in fact. But she doesn't have to worry about dealing with how the world feels about it because it's a secret that even her family and some of her friends don't know. Why has she kept it secret? Tamara likes having a really sexual relationship but also keeping it contained, so that people don't make a big deal about it and pigeonhole her. Keeping it secret and a segmented part of her life lets her focus on her work, see her wide circle of friends, and maintain a close friendship with her ex-husband and adult kids. It also fits the interests of her lover. "He's forty-five. He was married. He's not married now. I'm not sure what happened, but he said it had nothing to do with us. But I like keeping it contained, and if everybody knew, it might bleed into other parts of my life."

Tamara sees her lover once every ten days or so. They sometimes go out to dinner, but most of the cooking they do is in bed. Rather than longing for more, this arrangement is just what she wants. "I'm very comfortable with the way it is. I'm glad he comes, and I'm also glad when he goes because I have a busy life, too. I work full-time. I do freelance. I never intend to retire. I love what I do. I do calligraphy. I love my art, my home. I love my family. I love my granddaughter. It's like it's all come together. I'm not looking for an emotional attachment, although there is a warmth; we care about one another. But I'm not looking to be attached permanently to someone or to live with someone, so I think that's very freeing. It is what it is."

Tamara and her lover knew each other for a long time as colleagues, which created a lot of time for the sexual tension between them to build. "He's very flirtatious but probably with everyone because he's a very sexual guy. And I just called him on it one day. I said, 'You know, we banter like this back and forth, but if you're serious, I'm interested.' And we went up on the roof, and he talked to me and he kissed me, and that was that. It was almost five years ago."

And after a lifetime of often feeling more sexual than her partners, Tamara feels like she's finally met someone really sexually compatible. "He's probably the most sexual person I've ever been with. We can do anything we want. So we're very well matched, and he tells me so. At first I thought 'Oh, my God, he's young and I'm old,' but . . . there's a great deal of freedom, and that's probably because we're evenly matched."

But when Tamara suspected that he was having sex with another woman she stopped seeing him, not out of jealousy but out of fear, because they had had unprotected sex. "So I said, 'I expect you should see other people, but I also care about myself, and I need to take care of myself.' And he, of course, said there wasn't anybody else, but I don't know how truthful people are with one another. I said, 'Well, if you want to get back together and have protected sex, then that's fine.' And now we're back together. He'd rather not [have protected sex], but he wants to have me in his life, which is very empowering because, you know, to have anyone want to come back and be with you—especially someone who's a good deal younger—is empowering. It makes me feel like I'm damn good. And I know that already, but to have someone else think the same way makes you feel that much better.

"It's definitely the happiest time of my life," Tamara says. "Because I've gradually come to know who I am. All I know is that my mother died when she was sixty-seven, and she was sick with so many things, and she was old. She didn't have the education or the opportunities that I've had. At sixty-nine I probably feel younger than she did when she was forty."

GOING INTO THE UNKNOWN

Nina, sixty, a woman with fine features and a shock of closely cropped white hair, is also willing to take chances in her romantic/sexual life. A divorced mother of two, she moved from the suburbs to the city when her kids were grown to work as a photographer and filmmaker and to live a life that more closely reflected her artistic interests. A tango aficionado, she loves both the intense physicality and the adventure that each new partner brings. One night at a tango club, Nina started to dance with a handsome intriguing stranger and learned just how far physical chemistry and rhythm can take you. They danced every song together without saying a single word until the club closed. In fact, they couldn't speak. It turned out he was Swiss and could only communicate a couple of textbook phrases in English.

At four in the morning, they kissed good-bye on a street corner. Having gotten Nina's business card, however, he soon e-mailed her, and with the help of translation software invited her to visit him in Geneva.

Surprised at the invitation, Nina debated how far she should take this exciting but brief encounter. "I decided to go but told him that I'd only stay a few nights. I thought maybe I'd visit for a weekend; he was working and maybe I would travel in Italy. He said, 'What would you like me to bring?' And I said, 'A rose.' And he did. He picked me up at the airport with a rose, and we went to have coffee at this beautiful lakeside café. He drove this smart little American sports car. And then we walked in this charming little town outside of Geneva. Then we went back to his apartment. It was a wonderful apartment. It had a terrace that overlooked a church and the countryside. It was in an area that was ex-urban. It must have been a farming community at one point. And he made lunch, and his son was invited. And he grilled. And his son left. He was adorable. I have a picture. He was a few years younger than I. Divorced as long as I. And after lunch I remember helping him clear the plates and all of a sudden we were necking and in bed. And I remember asking him if he wanted to have intercourse. He said, 'Of course!'

"In the morning, there was a lot of sex, and at one point he said, "You know, we've become lovers.' I couldn't much figure out what he did for a living, but I think he ran production in a factory. I think he was college educated. He was clearly an athlete; he skied. He had very few books in his house, a lot of art.

"There were sunsets, rides up mountains while he slept in the sun as I wandered through the skiers' church. I'd write him a letter each morning using the French dictionary to communicate where I'd be going and when I'd return. We had this intense, sexual week together. He was into spanking. He liked to spank me, but he was just playing. He was clear he was just playing. And when I left it was sad. And the day before I left he said, 'I will see you; this isn't the end.' But what ended up happening is 9/11 happened within days of my return. He wrote sporadically, but he lost his job and could never find work again. And we ultimately lost touch."

Nina looks back fondly on the trip, but it's one of many. Her life is about experimenting, about letting things evolve, whether it's her photography, traveling to remote places, or meeting lovers. "For me life has always been an adventure." As an athlete who bikes through the city, Nina is open and ready for the twists and turns in the road in the years to come.

MIX AND MATCH

Just as ready to embrace life as Nina is Elizabeth, seventy-four, who married young and got pregnant right away but now is involved with two men. With a domineering husband there wasn't much adventure in her life when she was younger, particularly sexual adventure. After repeated failures to get her husband to go to therapy or to work on improving their marriage, with her three children grown, she finally got the courage to leave him. He was clearly not willing to change, and after years of feeling lonely Elizabeth longed for a real connection and exciting sex life.

She met a man at a spiritual workshop she was attending in California and had a relationship for eight years. It wasn't everything she wanted, but it was an improvement. He was able to give her the kind of emotional support her husband hadn't, but it wasn't as sexual as she would have liked. When that broke up Elizabeth was forced to face the reality that many men her age and older just don't have the same level of sexual energy she has. Others had the stamina but not the same interests. Elizabeth didn't set out to date two men simultaneously, but when it became clear that she might have to do that to get her needs met, she was open to it. After a lifetime of bending to someone else's will and playing by society's rules, she was ready to grab whatever life had to offer her.

"I'm seeing two men right now. I've been seeing Charlie for a year and a half. He's eighty years old and we're good company for each other and I enjoy him, but there hasn't been . . . much sexual activity there, and he's content with just being a companion." They go to the symphony, go out to eat, talk. "He comes to my house, and we sleep together and hug and so forth, but there's no actual sexual relationship. But I met another man, George, last summer who is only in his sixties and really interests me sexually. So he comes to see me once a week. It's a sexual relationship although we're becoming friends, too. It's not just sexual. I call it a 'supplemental relationship.' What I don't get from the one, I get from the other, so I still see Charlie on the weekend." We asked Elizabeth if these men knew about each other. "George [the younger guy with whom I'm having a more sexual relationship] knows about Charlie. He doesn't know any details, but he knows there's another man. But I haven't told Charlie about George because I just don't know how far this is going to go. I've told Charlie that I'm interested in a more sexual relationship, and he said that would be all right but he'd sorta like to know about it. But I haven't been able to tell him about that yet."

Not only is this Elizabeth's first time having two partners at once, it's also the first time she's gone after someone she wanted. In the past she always played a more passive role, responding to men who pursued her. Elizabeth says, "This time, with George, I initiated it, which is something I've never done. I went after him." He works on the grounds of the hospital where Elizabeth had been recuperating from hip surgery. She went back with the express purpose of seeing him and trying to get something started. "I was glad to be able to do that because that's not my nature to be that way. I was [finally] willing to take risks. That's one of the things I've been working on in my therapy: fear of rejection. And he made it easy for me because it appeared to me that he really was interested in me, too. But it's huge for me to be able to do that and not worry about being rejected. I mean, it's like, you know, you're seventy-three years old and you're still a teenager inside. I guess those feelings, we have them all our lives, don't we? But I think part of the reason I'm taking risks now is my age. My time's really running out. How much longer am I gonna have? I don't feel like I need a man to complete myself. I feel pretty secure, but I want to experience a complete sexual relationship, which I've never really had with any of the men that

I've been with. And George is still very virile, very capable of having a strong sexual relationship, and I just wanted that. I think that that's the bottom line.

"I've gone out after it because I'm just a lot freer. I used to worry about what people thought of me, you know, am I doing this right, am I doing that right? I've learned to be a little more centered and independent and be on my own."

SHARE-A-MAN

For Joani, seventy, going after what she wants and being in an alternative relationship is hardly something new. Since 1977, when she started the sex-positive, feminist Good Vibrations sex-toy shop in San Francisco, radical sex politics have always been in the forefront of her thoughts. This hasn't changed for her with age. Age has only afforded her more time to reflect.

Joani is currently in a share-a-man relationship. "Three years ago I met somebody at an intimacy workshop with whom I've been in a relationship pretty much since the weekend we met. But it has never been an exclusive relationship, and for most of the time we've been together he's also had another relationship that is of equal importance to him. I, on the other hand, have continued to do sexually all the things I did before I met him but at a significantly slower pace, because a large measure of my relationship energy has gone into my relationship with him. I'm not much for labels, but I kind of like the label *polyamorous*." One of the reasons that Joani likes the term *polyamory* is that it conveys the idea that there's enough love to go around and that no one has to get hurt in the process. For her it's about being open to having multiple relationships with the knowledge and consent of all partners rather than with deception.

However you define it, after not having a long-term lover for many years, Joani has enjoyed both the sex and the intimacy. "This relationship has been really nice. I've loved having a regular boyfriend and seeing him a lot. We care about one another a great deal, and sex with him is really good. He's introduced me to some sexual activities that I never participated in before. In particular, I really enjoy being dominated by him. His dominance over me is very light and, for the most part, is more psychological than it is physical. I speak very little or not at all when we are playing sexually, which is highly unusual for me. And I've found myself a good deal more relaxed about receiving pleasure than I used to be."

But being in an open relationship is not without real challenges. The other woman Joani shares her partner with, who knows about Joani, has been unwilling to work out the issues she has had with Joani, and it has caused tension.

"In my current situation, open communication all around isn't happening. Though I've repeatedly let my partner and his other partner (indirectly) know that I'm open to much more communication than we have had for the last three years, it's simply not to be with this particular combination of people. This is one of several reasons I'm finding it necessary to pull back and make room for others.

"In the future if I enter into another open relationship it will be a deal breaker for me if any one of the people involved refuses to communicate with me or with others in whatever combination of relationships we are in. I don't need to be a lover or even a friend of my lover's lover(s), but I have to be able to communicate with him, her, or them from time to time, especially to work out differences and conflicts should they arise. So these days I'm seeing him less frequently to make myself emotionally and physically available for a new partner or partners. I'm also committed to learning how to better enjoy my own company; that doesn't come easily for me."

SAVING THE BEST FOR LAST

It took Dell, eighty-four, many years to break out of her own shameful feelings about sex, and many more to deal with a late marriage and divorce that meant she was not going to have a traditional lifestyle that included children. Dell had sex with a woman for the first time when she was forty-eight. Up until that point in her life she had always found the idea of having sex with a women unappealing. But she credits the women's movement with changing her attitude because it "shifted my perception to seeing women as being as powerful as men," and that shift made her see women in a totally new light. Dell told us, "They say power is the greatest aphrodisiac. You know, women want to marry powerful men because they get power through their man. But if women could see themselves as powerful beings, then maybe they could be attracted to people whether they be man or woman." For her the crossover late in life was an empowering, freeing experience. Being with a woman "was far more sexual, the closeness, the touching . . . there was more of a sensuous kind of experience. Most of the men just yearn to fuck right away; that doesn't give a woman time enough. Women can take their time and caress each other and stimulate each other, and there's no penetration or else there is penetration with fingers and dildos."

Dell met a dark-haired beauty within a couple of years and fell in love. The relationship was deeply emotional and sexual. Already in her fifties, she thought she'd finally met her life partner. Tragically her new love was diagnosed with cancer and died within a few years. But the experience of being with women has expanded the possibilities open to Dell since then. "The fact that I'm bisexual certainly gives me more choices in my life." Dell's now open to finding either a male or female partner, seeing sexuality as spiritual, the important element being deep connection, not gender.

Dell's experience illustrates that our sexuality doesn't have to stagnate. It can change, evolving and opening new possibilities. Sometimes it takes decades to recognize the full array of options in front of us. Dell thinks that once more women open up to the possibility of being with women, the dimensions of the partner gap will completely change. "I think if older women were more open to having relationships with other older women that there would be [fewer] lonely women and more joyous women and . . . God, it just would be great . . . to see older women truly celebrating the fact that they are still in touch with their sexual nature. Because I think it's a huge part of the pleasures of being alive."

Whether it's the thrill of dating a man forty years younger, getting involved with a man who has an open relationship with another woman, or being with a woman for the first time, all of these women are exploring their options, expanding and testing relationship roles that fit their individual needs. This takes confi-

dence, creativity, and an openness to change. Betty, Nina, Elizabeth, Joani, and Dell have each trailblazed unique ways to fill the
partner gap that other women will be able to use as models as
they age. In the process these women are revolutionizing sexual
roles and showing us that age, far from making us staid and complacent, can actually make us more daring, more playful, and
more alive.

5.

TAKING YOUR SWEET TIME:

SEX AS WE AGE

When we talk about *sex,* it typically means something very specific. Often the word is merely used as a synonym for penetration. In Hollywood cinema, the quintessential sex scene usually involves two beautiful young actors earnestly pumping away at each other without much foreplay. But despite being the predominant image of sexual ecstasy, by itself the old "in-and-out" doesn't succeed in getting most women off.

As Betty describes with playful sarcasm, "For the most part when people think of sex they visualize a penis and a vagina, and it does this [*mimics a grade-school interpretation of sex*]. That's procreative sex. The vagina isn't even our sex organ; it's the birth canal. You don't think of a penis and a clitoris. That would make more sense. So what is sex? How do we define what sex is?"

First of all, not all sex is between men and women. But beyond the gender of sexual partners, as Betty says, "It isn't just about sexual intercourse or fucking or sucking. Sex has so much more possibility." As we grow older our bodies do change, altering some of the ways we approach sex. But no longer being able to go at it with furious pace can open up more intimate, varied, and satisfying forms of lovemaking.

A new field of healthy sex for older people is emerging. Far from being geriatric in style, it involves all kinds of intimate and imaginative play. And the wonderful thing is, for women who keep having sex throughout their entire lives, their bodies keep providing them with pleasure, sometimes more than they've ever had before.

In a 1998 survey by the National Council on Aging, 70 percent of women over fifty reported feeling freer, more relaxed with their bodies, and more able to laugh and have fun. Without a doubt, broadening our ideas about sex is a huge opportunity for increasing sexual excitement, intimacy, and pleasure—not just for older women but for everyone.

SEX VISION: 20/20

Most of the women we interviewed reported having a much clearer idea of what they want from sex now and what it means to them. For Ruth, whose husband, Harry, shares her sexual appetites, sex has become more nuanced and affected by emotions and thoughts as she's grown older. She says, "My sexual feelings and my sexual anticipation are much more thorough mind and body than they ever used to be. I mean, the sex now— it's in my head, it's in my boobs, in my pussy, and in my feelings, in my emotions. I think years ago it was just down there or in my breasts. It was just in my sexual organs, and it wasn't as infused throughout me.

"But sex is also very different now in my sixties than it was in my twenties, thirties, and forties. First of all, while I certainly still have all this desire, hormonal or physical or whatever, I am not as driven. It's not as imperious an event or demand as it was when I was younger, and that's good. It's more fun now, more relaxed, more spontaneous. Y'know, we get into bed at night and fool around and feel like doing it. We do it and it has to do with caring about each other and touching each other and obviously feeling the urges as well. So, yeah, it's very different. It doesn't have the intensity, although I must say I have had some really intense orgasms."

With more than eight decades of life to reflect on, Frances experiences sex as a combination of emotions, thoughts, and sensations. "The truth is that it takes your head, your heart, and your hands in order to consummate good sex and good social relationships." According to Frances, another difference between sex at eighty-six and sex earlier in life is lifestyle. "When I was younger, my husband and I had our own little house, with our own little bedroom, with our own little children, with our own little schedules for doing things. We tended to have sex at night, because we were busy working during the day. It's different now, because my partner comes [to the nursing home] in the daytime. We're not together at night, and so our sex therefore is an afternoon matinee. And the fact that we are older, we're more measured in what we want. We know how to pleasure each other directly now, as my husband and I did not necessarily know then. The pleasure is different because the body is different. Not better or worse but different."

SLIP AND SLIDE:
LUBRICATION KNOW-HOW

One of the biggest misconceptions about sex and the aging body is that women will definitely experience vaginal dryness and become less responsive. While vaginal dryness can become an issue with age, it's also a problem that can be easily solved with a little understanding and preparation.

First of all, if she is sexually excited a woman can become wet at any age. According to Extension Specialist Kathy Bosch, older women respond to sexual stimulation in the same way that younger women do, it just takes a little longer. Bosch says, "As women age, there will be a delay in lubrication development, but sexual play for one to five minutes will assist in effective lubrication."[6] Of course, messing around for five minutes before sex will usually make it a more enjoyable experience at any age, so needing to take things a little slower isn't necessarily an inconvenience.

Second, vaginal dryness seems to be as much a side effect of abstinence as it is a condition of age. While dealing with different patients during gynecological visits, Dr. Peggy Polaneczky has noticed that vaginal dryness seems to be a much bigger problem for women who have sex infrequently. If women keep having sex, even into their much later years, their bodies keep responding. Women who continue to have sex on a regular basis throughout menopause say that they don't need to use lubricants during sex. In fact, women who have orgasms more regularly are less depressed, sleep better, and are less prone to becoming incontinent.

It can be fun to experiment with many lubricants, although this could also get expensive because they range in price from $10 to $100. The two major categories of lubricants are water based and silicon, both of which have slightly different textures and different benefits. The most commonly available brand is probably the water-based lubricant K•Y Jelly, which you can buy in most drugstores and grocery stores. Like all water-based lubricants, it is easily absorbed into the skin, which may make it feel more natural but also means that it doesn't last very long. For women who want a longer-lasting product they won't need to reapply, a silicon lubricant might be better. There are hundreds of brands of lube to choose from, available at sex shops and on the Internet.

Oils are also a great lubricant for sex, and they're convenient; you probably have a few in your kitchen already. Best not to use them if you have $200 Egyptian cotton sheets because oil stains can leave lasting memories long after the night has faded.

Replens is an over-the-counter vaginal moisturizer that many women seem to like. It forms a moist coating on the surface of vaginal cells, creating lubrication that lasts forty-eight to seventy-two hours.

Aloe vera gel is also a great lubricant and is very healthy for the vaginal walls as well as for the penis. Lily of the Desert makes certified organic aloe vera jelly with vitamins A, C, and E. It's sold at health food stores around the country, or go to:

www.heathtouch.com

www.holistic-on-line.com

www.freepatentsonline.com

Many women who have gone through dry spells with little or no sex find that they need a lubricant to help them get back into the swing of things. In this case, for women who have problems with vaginal dryness, there are many kinds of lubricants to choose from.

OPENING UP AGAIN: VAGINAL DILATORS

According to gynecologist Dr. Polaneczky, older women who have sex infrequently may find that the opening of their vagina gradually becomes smaller. As a result, sex can be painful. For patients with this problem Dr. Polaneczky recommends vaginal dilators, which help to enlarge the vaginal opening. Vaginal dilators are a set of plastic or silicon rods that start small and gradually become wider in diameter. Using dilators along with lubricant and vaginal estrogen will slowly increase the size of the vagina, making sex less painful and helping women to get back to a healthy sexual routine. However, Dr. Polaneczky warns that dilation should be performed as part of a gynecological exam. Women should not try to do it on their own; if done incorrectly it can tear the vaginal lining, and it's especially dangerous if performed without vaginal estrogen.

Vaginal estrogen comes in the form of a cream, a tablet, or a ring that can be inserted into the vagina, where it secretes low doses of estrogen into the vaginal mucus. Since very little of the estrogen is absorbed into the bloodstream, it seems to be a safer form of estrogen therapy, which can help with other effects that aging can have on the vagina by strengthening the vaginal lining, increasing lubrication, and increasing the vagina's elasticity.[7]

Touch and stimulation can also help tone the vagina. Other supplemental tools for keeping the opening and muscles of the vagina in shape are dildos and vibrators, which can be used alone or with a partner.

GOOD VIBRATIONS:
DILDOS AND VIBRATORS

In general, dildos and vibrators have a wonderful design principle: They are built for giving orgasms and for playing with how one might achieve them with the highest degree of satisfaction. It's hard to go wrong with something made to induce pleasure. And it's never too late to start experimenting with them.

Betty told us a story about a woman who came to one of her workshops who was never completely satisfied by sex with her husband. After many, many years, when she was already in her seventies, she decided to try solving the problem. Betty remembers, "[She] totally transformed her sex life with her husband with a vibrator." Once they started playing around with the vibrator during sex, they discovered that it gave her the extra stimulation that she'd always needed to have an orgasm. Sex became more passionate for both of them because their experience was more equal and the chance to experiment added electricity to the relationship.

Some women worry that introducing a vibrator or dildo into sex with their partner will seem like a threat, implying dissatisfaction or inadequacy. But, actually, if your partner is interested in your satisfaction, as Betty's experience shows, diplomatically giving him or her an extra key to your pleasure points will (in most situations) make things hotter for both of you.

FLYING HIGH: SWINGS

If there's some kind of physical injury, it's important to keep things light, not just metaphorically but also literally. Before Betty had hip-replacement surgery, she had a lot of trouble being comfortable during sex, and most positions were too much of a strain to be enjoyable. But she remembers how once, in a loft space in San Francisco, her partner came up with a creative solution to the problem. Betty recalls being "put in this swing. My legs were held suspended. I was lying there and it was total comfort, total comfort. I didn't have any stress, no pain. God, I never felt anything but comfort and sensuous, delicious feelings." By freeing her from pain, the swing allowed Betty to really let go.

Betty's hip surgery worked miracles for her. She's now basically pain free. But for people with ongoing disabilities, the effort to put in a swing could mean ongoing sexual enjoyment instead of pain. Of course, most homes don't come equipped with a swing, and in many cases it can be challenging to install. Even Betty, who would love to have a swing in her apartment, has resisted putting one in. But she says, "It would make sense for me to do it because I think they're wonderful."

There are also less drastic sexual props that can lessen the physical impact of sex. The love seat is another piece of sex furniture in which the woman can sit while the man stands. Or the woman can be propped up or tilted back or lifted, whichever is the most comfortable. Chairs and beds can also be used during sex to hold one's body in positions that are less strenuous and to keep pressure off injured body parts.

SAFE SEX: OLDER PEOPLE CAN ALSO CONTRACT STDS

While we associate aging with aches and pains, we associate youth with sexually transmitted diseases (STDs). But the fact is they don't end when you join AARP. Jane, sixty-three, told us she believes she contracted the human papilloma virus (which makes her more susceptible to cervical cancer) from her seventy-year-old lover. And according to recent statistics, 10 percent of HIV cases in the United States are men and women over fifty. For older women the statistics are even more serious: 18 percent of AIDS cases are women over fifty, and of this 18 percent, women of color represent the largest portion. AIDS cases among older women are increasing at nearly five times the rate as they did in 1995. Even more startling than the number of full-blown AIDS cases is the rate of HIV transmission, which has increased by almost 100 percent among women older than fifty.[8] As more older people continue to be sexually active later in life, and more of them have multiple sexual partners, the risks of contracting HIV and other STDs may continue to increase. Senior discounts clearly don't provide immunity.

But as anyone who has had to navigate sex since the 1980s can verify, this doesn't need to be an impediment to having a stimulating sex life. Education about safe sex is becoming more available in older communities because the reality is ALL women need to protect themselves.

BEYOND THE "IN AND OUT": EXPANDING THE POSSIBILITIES

Whereas women's sex drive can actually increase with age, many—even very healthy—men experience a loss of stamina and trouble maintaining an erection as they get older. For the always wild Harriet, seventy-nine, whose image and definition of sex is wedded to penetration, being with men her own age has no allure. She says, "Older men do not have any sex appeal for me because sex is life and it's youth. Sex and youth go together for me. Clitoral orgasms are great, but I'm not happy without penetration. The penetration is very important to me, and mutual orgasm—that's the peak, that's the most wonderful thing in life."

Although Harriet has had some wild experiences with younger lovers since she turned sixty, her insistence on youth and penetration has limited her options, making her feel sexually deprived of late. But for other women who are more open to different kinds of sex, and a wider age range, the biological changes their male partners face (or may face in the future) aren't a focus of concern. When Ruth talks about her sex life with her husband, Harry, she has a hard time equating her sexual satisfaction with his erections. "For men there sometimes is the difficulty having, getting, and maintaining an erection. But we've never had any of those problems. Or if he had a problem at his end, I was never that conscious of it because he would make efforts to, you know, satisfy me in other ways and vice versa."

Since Ruth and Harry have a varied sexual repertoire, it's no big deal if one specific method is unavailable. "I certainly think that oral sex on the part of both partners is another means of getting satisfaction. I mean, oral sex is an entity unto itself, one that you do when you're young and everything is at a level of ten, but certainly at a point when it may not be possible to do some of the usual things, I think that that's a way of accommodating and adjusting. You don't look at that as a loss; you simply look at that as, Okay we're not going to have that this evening, but we're going to have this."

Experimenting with new ways of satisfying your partner and being satisfied in return is crucial if one is going to adjust to the inevitable realities of aging. Joani, seventy, has dated several men who had trouble getting erections, and each time she made it clear that it wasn't a big deal. "I'm not dependent on their erections for my pleasure, and I say so. If he doesn't have reliable erections, but he's good with his hands and his mouth, and, more important, if he's attentive and loving towards me, so what if his erection comes and goes?"

Yet, no matter how open you are to manifold forms of sexual satisfaction, it may take patience and time to convince your partner. As Freddie learned when she started dating again in her sixties after her husband, Sidney, died, many men feel a huge amount of performance anxiety. Often, their own nervousness is the biggest factor. "Older men have a lot of sexual problems. The [men I was with] had a hard time having an erection or sustaining an erection, no matter how helpful I was to them. I think part of it was age; part of it was anxiety. I was a new partner. I think in a new situation it's easier for women than it is for men. I could feel anxiety, but that didn't prevent me from being able to be sexual. They felt anxiety, and it prevented them from being sexual."

A woman who makes it clear that she can be satisfied in different ways can relieve a man's performance anxiety, but this may also not be true. Elaine says, "Most men at my age level are having difficulties with erections and y'know they feel embarrassed by this and they try to make explanations for it and I just don't think all of that is necessary. I think that at our age we should realize that physically we are not what we were twenty or thirty years ago and that we should try to accept that and go on to another level, which could be heavy petting, or there are so many other ways to be gratified besides intercourse. But I think that many men (particularly the African-American men who I get involved with) haven't truly learned how to expand on love-making. My husband didn't even know what foreplay was. It was like one kiss and in it goes. But I've been known to have an orgasm just by the touch and the feel and the manipulation of my body. I really don't need you to go inside me to be sexually satisfied. I can be satisfied with someone caressing my body and y'know

AARP's 2004 study of sexuality showed that men had recurring issues with impotence and were far more likely than women their age to express dissatisfaction with their sex lives.

Men are also far more likely than women to have trouble as they age, as demonstrated by notably higher rates of depression and suicide. While the rate of depression for women does not increase with age, that for men does—by a whopping 500 percent. The odds of depression for childless divorced men aged seventy and older are more than twice as high as that for divorced childless women of that age group.

kisses and hugs and touching, and to me that's almost more important than the act itself."

In 1985, advice columnist Ann Landers asked her female readers, "Would you be content to be held close and treated tenderly and forget about the 'act'?" Of the ninety thousand readers who responded, 72 percent said yes, and interestingly enough, 40 percent of that group was under forty years old. The clear feedback is that closeness and touch are a huge part of what's so powerful about sex. When we asked Ellen, seventy-four, who has had an animated sex life with her partner, Dolores, if she could imagine giving up sex, she immediately made a distinction between sex and touch. She could only imagine giving up sex in the very limited capacity that it is usually discussed. "I think, in all honesty, *that* I could give up. The touching and the kissing and the physical closeness, no. I would waste away if I did not have that." Sex for her and Dolores, seventy-five, is now less about physical feeling than about the emotional link that they feel while being close to each other. "Our touching is just as much a part of our passion as having orgasms."

But men's insecurity about their sexual performance has led to major problems in Elaine's relationships, sometimes even causing them to end. "They pull away, and I think it's due to their embarrassment [over] not being able to perform like a young stallion. But it leaves me thinking, What is wrong with me? So it becomes discouraging, and I've kind of withdrawn now from dating because it just doesn't seem worth it to me. How will I ever build a relationship if men are just so shaky and unsure, and they are focusing on things that to me aren't important? We're not on the same wavelength, and you can't make things work all by yourself. To me there's nothing like communication between two people, especially if you see a problem arising."

KNOCK ON WOOD:
ERECTIONS AND VIAGRA

So what about Viagra? Viagra and other pharmaceuticals to correct erectile dysfunction are clearly in widespread use, but there are things to consider before taking it, starting with the fine print about health risks. Although Elaine wanted to make her relationship work and find a solution that would please both her partner and herself, she was wary of Viagra. "I was afraid of Viagra for my companion (who was having so many problems) because at that time it was just coming onto the market, and there were all these stories about heart attacks and this thing and that thing, and I didn't want to feel that I was a part of someone who took it and then had some kind of adverse reaction." But she also never broached the subject.

On the other hand, Stella, who met her lover in her late sixties through matchmaker Fay Goldman and started to have some of the wildest sex in her life, did. As Stella describes it, "I have a good, strong libido, and I'm always interested in sex. With him I got less self-conscious, 'cause he's not self-conscious at all in this area, and I was able to talk about sexual things with him: what I wanted, what I didn't want, what I liked. . . ." Since she was open about all the other aspects of her sex life she felt comfortable bringing up the use of Viagra, and her partner welcomed the suggestion. "You know, once in a while he doesn't get an erection, but it doesn't even matter. The sex is good. We cuddle. We kiss a lot. We're very physical. That's the area that we're the best in."

In fact, for Stella sex is the strongest aspect of their relationship. "It's the area that if I want to save the relationship I can always go there." Viagra, but maybe more important clear communication, has allowed Stella and her partner to keep their sex life charged.

Sharon (not her real name), sixty-one, another attractive, vivacious woman, who has spent a lifetime in the arts, has been married for thirty-six years, but she and her husband don't share an open sexual rapport. She loves him deeply, but their sex together has ceased to satisfy her. Part of the problem is that he, too, has trouble maintaining an erection, but Sharon has never felt she could admit that she is unsatisfied in any way, let alone suggest something like Viagra. She explained, "His pride is a big issue, and he just doesn't take any drugs anyway, even when he has a root canal. So that just isn't an option. I understand him too well. I mean, I could be wrong, but I don't think I'm wrong. So I just kinda pretend that the sex is better than it is, and I've been doing that for a long time.

"He can't get an erection nearly as quickly as he could, which is typical of men his age. It's harder to do, and it's harder to come when he gets one." Sharon understands that the decline in his sexual performance is fairly typical for a man his age and that there are various solutions to the problem. Yet despite their deteriorating sex life, she feels that her husband's fragile ego wouldn't be able to handle the challenge of dealing with the problem. Instead they go through the motions of sex the way they always have, without addressing any changes. "Maybe that's my fault and I should try and be more adventurous, but to be honest it's just not that much fun for me. I'm not sexually attracted to him anymore. So that's part of it, too. I love him. I'm not gonna leave him. I very much appreciate all of his good qualities, but I'm not sexually attracted to him anymore."

Sharon admits that some unresolved grievances she has had with her husband have driven a wedge into their physical intimacy. To make up for this lack in their relationship she masturbates instead, and in the past she's also had affairs. Despite the love and support that Sharon and her husband have for each other in many areas of their lives, they haven't been able to communicate to work through their sexual problems.

Even if Sharon's husband is opposed to pharmaceutical drugs like Viagra, which is obviously a legitimate option, there are plenty of other ways of dealing with erectile dysfunction. Cock rings, which fit onto the base of the penis and in many cases help sustain erections longer, are one solution. Others are oral sex and manual stimulation. There are vibrators and dildos to experiment with. It just takes some daring and an open line of communication on the part of both parties to explore the possibilities.

SEXUAL GROWTH

For some couples time spent together and knowledge of each other's bodies make their sex better. Connie's relationship and sex life with her husband, Antonio, have improved dramatically over time. "The first time I had sex with him (in my sixties) it was okay. It wasn't great or anything like that, but we continued to be attracted to each other and it became great. I think it was because we are at a different period in our life. Maybe everybody knows it, and we just didn't. I didn't know it before, that you adapt. It is something you make happen; it's not just like magic. You make it happen if you have the desire and the intention, and you find out how."

With time Connie and Antonio have learned to experiment with the best ways to please each other. These changes have not only improved their relationship but also keep it fresh and helps maintain their intense attraction. "Sometimes Antonio and I will go out to a movie, or I will see him walking down the street, and I'm always surprised there surges inside of me that same feeling when we first went to the movies together or the feeling when I saw him and thought, You know, he's pretty attractive."

WORKING AT IT

Often couples operate with the misconception that sex should just magically happen and that having a healthy, romantic relationship means that there's nothing to discuss or work on. Not only is this attitude unrealistic, but it also suggests that people don't change and desire doesn't evolve.

Our sex drive needs to be exercised in the same way the body needs to be exercised. According to Dr. Polaneczky, this includes opening up what you expect from sex. She says, "We have such predefined ideas about how it's supposed to be that we don't like it to be anything other than that and don't legitimize it any other way. We don't cut it any slack, the same way we cut other things in our life slack." She says if couples, whatever their age, always wait to feel desire they're going to have a lot less sex than they might want. How many of us need to be cajoled into going to the gym, or the movies, for that matter, and are really happy we've gone? Dr. Polaneczky likens it to a loop: You might not immediately have the desire to have sex, but once you do, you enjoy it, which makes you more likely to want to do it again.

As a culture we are increasingly geared toward self-improvement. We are willing to work on our physical appearance, our social skills, our diet, our work performance. As Dr. Polaneczky advises, "You can do the same thing with sex. And it's a lot more fun."

Variety is the spice of life, especially when it comes to sex. If we compare sex to a conversation, then it needs to build on itself. Even the most profound discussion will lose its charm and excitement if it is repeated verbatim for five nights in a row. In order to be intimate and fulfilling, sex needs to reflect our changing moods and desires. It also needs to adapt to the changes in our bodies that happen throughout our lives, especially in our later years.

6.

PARTY OF ONE:

SOLO SENSUALITY

There comes a time in every woman's life when she has to take matters into her own hands. Whether in a long-term relationship, with intermittent partners, or single, the person best able to know and meet a woman's sensual needs is often herself. Betty, seventy-eight, whose reputation as a sex expert is rooted in her legendary masturbation workshops for women of all ages, reports, "You don't need to have a partner to have orgasms. That's one of the biggest myths in America. Don't ever count on partner sex for sexual release, because it's going to be the least likely one [to] come through. It's the sex that you're having with yourself that will carry the day."

Masturbation can make partner sex more exciting and more pleasurable. This is as true at seventy as it is at thirty. Literally and figuratively speaking, masturbation is one of the few pleasures in life that is always at our fingertips.

The vast majority of the women we interviewed told us that

they feel that masturbation is an important part of being a sexual human being and a way of staying in touch with their sexual needs. Regardless of different lifestyles, circumstances, and beliefs, most find masturbation to be an empowering way of maintaining their sexuality and fulfilling themselves. Betty says, "One of the main reasons my sexuality has remained alive is that I love myself. I love masturbation." Elaine, eighty, says, "Thank God for it." Ruth, seventy-two, adds, "Masturbation has a life all its own. You know, no one knows what you like as much as you do." Harriet, seventy-nine, admits, "I still don't prefer it [but] thank God for these little vibrators. I mean, they're marvelous. I told you the slogan of the pocket rocket, right? We've put more women in orbit in a day than a man has in a year." Frances, eighty-six, adds with a mischievous smile, "How do I feel about masturbation? In one word, *good, very good.*"

Clearly, there's no age limit for enjoying masturbation, nor does the activity lose its excitement over time. Dell, eighty-four, says, "I just think there is nothing like having a great orgasm that opens you up and makes you feel like a liberated, breathing, pulsating human being. All I have to do is put my hand on my clitoris to feel desire. I masturbate on a fairly regular basis, depending on my energy and my health, but I try to wake up with it. I call it my sacred sex ritual. I feel it's very important to be in touch with your sexual nature. It's an important, life-sustaining energy."

Over the course of her life Dell has had many partners, and she is open to having more in the future, but she also feels that being single is an important exercise in self-satisfaction. She says, "I am presently not in a relationship. I am in what I am defining as a new lifestyle, which I have called self-sexuality [*laughs*]. My sexual activity is me, myself, and my vibrator. I would like to spend the next ten years treating myself as my own best lover. [And a part of this is] taking the best care of myself, which is something I've not really done. My concern has been [for] others, and now it has to be [for] myself."

Being one's own best lover should be an inspiring idea for everyone, whether single or in a relationship, young or old. Yet masturbation and self-exploration still go against many societal restrictions. If you are at a dinner party it's more acceptable to reveal a sexual exploit with a stranger than it is to admit to having a powerful sexual experience with oneself. As a result, not having a partner and having to rely on solo sexual satisfaction can be seen as shameful. This social bias is particularly detrimental to older women because demographics can make it harder for them to find partners.

SHAMELESS PLEASURES

The reality is that masturbation becomes more important, not less, for many women as they get older. Elaine told us, "I never gave it much thought as a young person, because I was just having sex and I was totally satisfied with that. But as I've gotten older, I'd say for the last ten years, I [have] found that these feelings, these yearnings, whatever you want to call them, were still present with me, and I began to masturbate. Oh, what a relief. What a relief!"

Elaine feels open and comfortable talking about her desires and physical needs. However, not all women her age (not all women, period) can talk about their sexual desires as openly. And many of Elaine's friends (mostly older churchgoing African-

American women like herself) grew up when there were even more sexual taboos, and masturbation was seen as a dirty secret that "nice women" didn't engage in. Elaine says, "I think masturbation is an okay thing. [But] my friends, oh my goodness, they throw up their hands at it. But I'm sure they've thought about it. Maybe they don't know how to go about it, you know, to pleasure themselves. But I do."

Harriet, who declares proudly that "sex is the core of my life," told us, "I think I'm very different from women of my generation, very different." When she tries to talk about sex with friends her age, many, though not religious like Elaine's friends, insist that it's unnecessary. It's hard for them to admit that they think about sex, let alone actually get them to speak about their thoughts and experiences. In a group talk with four other women at the summer cottage she rents every August in Cape Cod, Massachusetts, Harriet tried to break down this conversational barrier and asked a group of her friends if they still thought about sex. Most said that they never did. Only Lori, an elegant eighty-year-old German-born friend and a widow, would admit to still feeling sexual desire. Lori said, "My lifetime commitment is gone, but my body still has needs." Instantly, a second woman in the group attacked her, saying, "I don't buy that. The brain is stronger than the body." "You feel I shouldn't have needs now?" Lori asked. "I think you shouldn't concentrate on them," the woman retorted.

Harriet feels that this conversation is typical of what some women of her generation think about sex and their needs as women and is due in large part to the fact that they were taught as children to fear their sexuality. Harriet told us that when she was little she wasn't allowed to sleep with her hands under the blanket. At the time, she didn't understand the reason for this strange nighttime rule, but it nevertheless had a huge impact on her. "When I was a kid my mother had us so freaked out about sex. I mean, it was really absurd. The apartment would be freezing in the middle of winter. When we were asleep she'd come and check to be sure that our little hands were not inside our blanket, and if they were she'd pull our hands out. She was afraid we'd play with ourselves. And I guess it got to me somehow, because as a young person, as a teenager I never did it. Never masturbated."

That was the 1940s. Since then, attitudes about sex have improved, and the discourse about sexuality is opening up. But it's been a long haul. Dell recalls buying her first vibrator at Macy's in the 1970s. In contrast with the sex-toy distributors we have now, in shops and on the Internet, in 1974 the only place for a woman to buy a vibrator was at a department store, where it was sold as a body massager, not something strictly for sexual pleasure. Dell was already an accomplished businesswoman in her forties, but she was still mortified. "When I asked the salesperson where they sold the body massagers, he said, 'What do you want to use it for?' That really stopped me in my tracks. I was just aghast. I was shocked. I couldn't answer for a moment until I caught my breath and then I said, 'To massage my back, of course.' Because, you know, most people bought body massagers to massage their backs. Then he told me where to go, where they sold them. I don't think he was trying to be snotty. I think they made different appliances for different parts of the body. But to me it was very embarrassing.

"I finally got to the row where they had them. I can't remember the others. I just remember seeing the Magic Wand lying straight out of its package. It was hooked into an outlet. People could pick them up and put them on, so people could see what they felt like. I'm not sure if this is something that they still do today, but they did in 1972 or 1973. So I picked up the Magic Wand, and I turned it on. It had two speeds, a high and a low, and I'm not sure what speed I got first, but anyway it sounded *awfully* loud to me and I thought, 'Oh, my God, everybody's hearing that, and everybody on the floor knows what I want to use it for!' Oooooooohhhh, that guilt."

Dell's experience buying a vibrator took on the significance of a shameful confession, a public admission of her intention to masturbate. Not only was masturbation socially unacceptable, but there was hardly any acknowledgment that such things as sex toys and erotic vibrators even existed. "I don't know if we even had the name *sex toy*. That language came later. But I've always thought, Why do they call it a toy? It's such an important thing to be called a toy." However, the humiliating experience of buying a vibrator at Macy's turned Dell into a sexual pioneer.

"[I realized] that, jeez, all these other women have to go through this experience just to pick up the Magic Wand, be exposed to these questions. Wouldn't it be a good idea for somebody to open up a place that sells them directly for women?" Dell decided to create Eve's Garden, a store that sells sex-education books and videos as well as sex toys. Instead of putting women in the embarrassing, secretive mission of pretending that they were using vibrators for backaches or foot massages, Dell wanted to create a place that was empowering and informative. Eve's Garden was a first. Dell says, "I was the first who catered to women exclusively. At that time there were two stores in existence. One was called the Pleasure Chest and the other the Pink Pussy Cat in the Village. [But] it was a little intimidating for women to walk in because it wasn't that comfortable. So I was the first that catered to women and also the first to have literature that encouraged women to be orgasmic and to masturbate."

Thirty years later Dell no longer works daily at Eve's Garden, though she is involved in publicity, buying new products, and writing the company's literature. But one of her great pleasures was always helping women who came into the store: "Oh, yeah, I loved that. There was the time that a woman came into the store, this was in 1980, and she banged her fists down on the counter and she said, 'I've been married for twenty years and I've had four children and I've never experienced an orgasm and I want you to sell me anything you can to help me enjoy my body.'"

But Dell says to this day only about 10 percent of the women who come in are over sixty. "Probably a lot of women are more shy about it because of their older age and because [they] have been indoctrinated to feel that sex is not necessarily that important in their life, and so they say, 'Sex is sort of past for me.' They just give up. That's why your film and book will be important. It will hopefully rev up older women."

Today, thirty years after the opening of Eve's Garden, it is still a special place, but now there are other sex shops that also are sensitive to women's needs. And older women who have the gumption to walk into a sex shop are most often met with sensitivity. That's good because many of us, young and old, still find buying a "sex toy" and admitting to the fact that we really like sex and

masturbation embarrassing. Shelley, sixty-six, told us about buying a dildo for the first time in her sixties. "It was very funny. I
was with a friend of mine, married friend, dear friend I've known
since I was a kid, and we're out to dinner one night and I told her
how I was feeling and how I miss sex, and I said, 'I know there's a
shop near here so would you come with me?' I wouldn't go by
myself, and she shocked me because she's pretty conservative,
but we went in together and of course it's a little uncomfortable, a
little embarrassing, but all I wanted was a dildo. And she's looking on the shelf, and she's helping select. Well, of course, because
she wasn't buying it for herself it was much easier, and then this
gentleman came over and said, 'Can I help you?' And I then told
him what I was looking for so he points to [a smallish one], and I
said, 'No. If I'm going to get one, I want a big one!'" So even
though she was embarrassed Shelley ultimately mustered up the
courage to ask for what she really wanted.

Betty started her masturbation workshops in the 1960s because
of her belief that the key to great sex is having an intimate relationship with your own body. Beyond that, Betty believed that in
order for women to really feel entitled to the same rights and
social status as men, women needed to shift their attitudes toward
sex, to pay more attention to their own sexual pleasure, to be able
to talk about it, and be proud of it. Betty's orgasm workshops
were the antithesis of a knitting circle or a Tupperware party.
Revolutionary for the time, her syllabus still would be considered radical by many.

    She recently stopped running the workshops. But how many
women today don't know what their own genitals look like or

how to fully pleasure themselves? Betty's workshops, where twenty-year-olds sat next to seventy-year-olds, were designed to address that. Betty started each workshop session with the same question: "What is your relationship to your body and your orgasms?" Then she took each student on a guided tour of her own pleasure source. "At the end of the first day we did genital exams because I'd found out that women had not, were not, looking at their own pussies. They didn't know what they looked like. Or if they did look, they thought they were ugly or horrible. Then I did a guided masturbation ritual where I'd start off guiding them through different standing positions, kneeling positions, how to use a vibrator, flex their pc (pubococcygeus) muscle. And then I would call an erotic recess, and everyone did their own."

Betty remembers one older woman in particular who had a really powerful experience at the workshop. "She was in her eighties, and she had breast cancer. She was dying; she knew she didn't have much longer to live. She was a Mormon and she'd been an old maid and she'd never had an orgasm and she wanted to have one before she died. So the whole group got behind her, I mean, energetically. And she did!"

The fact that Betty is seventy-eight and still living a dynamic and sexual life, dating a man forty-plus years her junior, is the biggest testament to the effectiveness of her teaching philosophy. But masturbation became particularly important to her personally when she started going through menopause in her fifties. In fact, looking back now, she feels that it saved her sex life. Her body was changing; it wasn't that her drive was gone; but it was different. For one thing, partner sex didn't seem like an option. "Vaginal penetration was blah." It was too rough on her vaginal lining, which was thinning because of hormonal changes. Betty didn't want her sex life to end, nor did she think that it would be healthy to stop having orgasms, but there was no external support or reassurance for dealing with what was happening to her. She got the clear social and medical message that menopause might well be the end of her sexuality. Betty assessed the situation and realized that if she wanted to keep her sex drive alive and pumping, she needed more consistent stimulation. "The thing is, use it or lose it . . . and I wasn't about to lose it." Considering her options, Betty went with the things at hand. "I had my vibrator and my clitoris, and these two things were plenty."

Betty started to masturbate on a regular basis. The more attention she gave to her sexual arousal, the more she realized how hard it was to find quality erotic material. She liked to watch porn for the visual stimulation, but the background music was cheesy and distracting. So she got creative, turned the sound off, and played her own music to create porn that really turned her on. Over time she felt her sexual desire becoming stronger and stronger.

By the time that menopause ended for Betty, she had regained her sexual drive and was ready for something new. "I went through all of these different stages, and I'd pretty much done everything. I had now gotten into my sixties. I was having some pain in my hip [Betty later had hip replacement; see Chapter 7], but I was trying to figure out, you know, what's next? What would I want to do? What would turn me on? What would be interesting? And I thought, Heterosexual fucking. Having sex with a man again. That would be very interesting. Because I had this big long time away from it." Rather than having experienced menopause and the attendant changes in her body as a period of sexual deprivation, Betty remained sexually spirited through masturbation. And ultimately her body was totally prepared for the work-out that her much younger lover would give her.

Even now, in her relationship with Erik, Betty makes sure that masturbation is part of her weekly routine. She jokes about pen-ciling it into her busy schedule, but underneath her lighthearted attitude, her commitment to herself and her sexual routine is very serious. "Once I started living with Erik I became too reliant on partner sex, because it feels good and you get a bigger orgasm. But what happens is, as the time goes on and you have less part-ner sex, instead of filling in with masturbation, you're now going to wait for the next partner sex. So it's like I have turned my sex drive over to my partner. This is what I think women do with men. They'll have sex when he gets around to it or he initiates it or whatever." But if women remember that masturbation is an important part of sexuality and not a second-rate option, plea-sure is always at hand, whether we're in relationships or not.

Raquel (not her real name), an earthy Latina with a warm laugh, has been involved with her lesbian lover for more than twenty years. Patricia (also a pseudonym), her partner, says that after all this time she still feels a thrill when Raquel comes home. And when you see them together it's clear that the warmth and fire go both ways. But Patricia, an intense, political filmmaker who has been a wonderful and faithful partner, is no longer interested in sex. Her desire seems to have slipped away, and other than feel-ing some guilt toward her lover she really feels no loss. We asked Raquel, who still feels intense sexual desire, how she handles this change in their life, and her response was practical. After twenty years she and Patricia have created a home, a life, a group of friends. As two filmmakers they sometimes work together. They still cuddle and kiss, and Raquel isn't ready to give any of that up. She also feels that pushing her partner to engage in sex when she doesn't have the desire feels almost abusive. So how does she handle it? Masturbation and dance. Through regular masturbation, a deep connection to her orgasmic self, and regular, very intense dance classes, where she sweats, lets out steam, feels the rhythm of the music, and moves her body sexually, Raquel has managed to maintain her beloved relationship with her partner without sacrificing her sexual self.

Sarah (also a pseudonym), eighty-five, hasn't had a partner in decades, but unlike Raquel she reports that until recently her sexuality had pretty much subsided. A lively octogenarian and musical historian, she still works and sees her grandchildren, children, and friends regularly. She wasn't thinking about her sexuality much, but a few years ago it was resurrected through masturbation and fantasy. Sarah was having problems sleeping, and she found her thoughts drifting to her old lovers, of which there had been many. "A game spontaneously developed in my mind," she recalls. She started graphically remembering her sexual encounters with lovers, but, since she had been more inhibited as a younger woman, she started editing her memories. What emerged were graphic fantasies in which she coached her past lovers with all the force and clarity she had lacked as a younger woman to give her exactly what would pleasure her. What started as a way to help her sleep has turned into a full-blown sexual life, filled with powerful sexual scenarios that truly turn Sarah on. In the process Sarah realized that her capacity to feel pleasure and be orgasmic hadn't diminished. Just like Betty, she just needed to find a way to get turned on and stimulate herself, and her mind led her to a great source.

SOLO SENSUALITY IS MORE THAN JUST MASTURBATING

It isn't just that we don't stimulate ourselves sexually. If we're alone it can be hard to do all the things we would if we had partners. Carmen, sixty-four, a former dressmaker with a timeless sensuality, a well-proportioned body, and a sassy Latina playfulness, is now recovering from cancer. But despite her illness, expressing her sexuality still means going out and having fun, whether she has a partner to bring along or not. Carmen likes to take herself on dates: to the movies, to dinner, dancing, sometimes even to male strip clubs. She explained to us that as she moved into her fifties she started to go out more by herself. "[I got to the point where if] I wasn't dating anybody, I felt, 'Why should I lock myself behind these closed doors?' I mean, I had a job. I was working. So I said, 'I will go to dinner by myself.' And on Saturdays, if I don't feel like cooking, I'll get pretty and go out to dinner."

As far as Carmen is concerned there's no big difference between being sexy at twenty and being sexy at seventy. "I find that men are very sexy, and I love men that are still sexual. I want to be sexually attractive to them. I love to wear sexy clothes. I've always been a very sexy woman. Even when I'm home I wear my little short things. I like to look cute. Even if I'm just going [shopping], and if somebody tells me I'm looking good . . . oh, I know I'm looking good."

Carmen trusts that wherever she goes she won't be alone. "You meet so many people. When you go out by yourself and say to yourself, 'I'm not going to meet anybody,' is when you meet all kinds of friends. When I go dancing I sit at the bar and socialize, and you meet ladies and you meet men. You dance. I never had problems with that. You know, my children say, 'Why do you do that?' I say, 'What do you want me to do?'"

Staying in touch with and expressing their desire has enabled many of the women we talked to to see their sexuality outside the conventional "relationship box." And, at times, savoring the sensual pleasures of the world has been an exciting solo adventure. As Betty points out, "Who says everything has to come in pairs? What is this, Noah's ark?"

At times when partner sex is infrequent, masturbation is a way of keeping vaginal muscles toned. And each orgasm increases our muscle memory, making it easier and faster to repeat the experience. Sexual fantasies give us a place to explore many aspects of who we are, those we would want to play out with another person and those we wouldn't. Masturbation can be simple or highly complex, with all the different physical, emotional, and psychological factors involved. Trying to explain one of her recurring sexual fantasies to us, Dell finally exclaimed, "Ooooh, the psyche is so complicated!"

Desire continually changes and renews itself, so there's always something new to look forward to. Masturbation is a way of exploring, owning, and taking control of the evolving landscape of our desires.

Dell says, "I think it's up to women to feel good and positive about themselves as sexual beings and not be inhibited and restrained by society. If women aren't fully able to express their sexuality, then it keeps them down, energy-wise and creative-wise. As an older woman, I hope to be a sexual being till the day I die."

7.

BODIES BUILT TO LAST:
OUR BODIES OVER TIME

LIVING IT UP INSTEAD OF
GIVING IT UP

We tend to focus on the negative aspects of aging, the slow but irreversible path of our body's decline. Yet, as medicine and nutrition continue to advance, the experience of aging is also rapidly changing. While the process clearly isn't without challenges, it doesn't have to be a downhill slope either. The medical possibilities for repairing the body have never been greater. More and more older women are leading active lifestyles, and some are enjoying their bodies more than ever before.

When Shelley, sixty-six, walks into a room she brings intense energy with her. "I am a day-to-day person, and life to me is very exciting." Shelley is the executive director of an affiliate of the National Employment Lawyers Association. Addressing employment discrimination is a flourishing area of the legal field, and in addition to being stimulating, Shelley's work keeps her in contact with a huge number of people, many of them much younger than she. But Shelley attributes her health and vitality largely to exercise. "It's sort of my life's blood. It always has been and hopefully always will be. I exercise four or five days a week. I do like an hour, an hour and a half, depending on the day, and if I don't have time I'll try to do at least a half hour."

Increasing numbers of studies of older women (and men) emphasize the extraordinary health benefits of exercise. It reduces the chances of developing heart disease, breast cancer, and depression.[9] It helps to lower high blood pressure, build bone density, and control weight. Exercise also raises energy levels, increases self-confidence, and improves balance. As Shelley says, "It's key. It's key for my emotional as well as physical well-being."

Although Shelley's exercise routine isn't as demanding as it used to be, she's committed to staying in shape. "There are many mornings I push myself. I'm a little tired. I really don't feel like going, but I would never allow myself to give in to that. I work out in my building, which is fabulous. [I do] the elliptical machine, treadmill, weights, upper-body machines, abs—not so much abs, I let those go a little—but mostly cardio. Once I'm finished, of course I'm thrilled I did it, and I have much more energy, much more energy to go through my day, feeling attractive and confident and emotionally good. I still think I look pretty good, you know? I mean, I can look at myself and feel that I'm doing the best to keep myself healthy and vital and energized. And to me it's really important how I feel, not necessarily how others perceive me."

For Ruth, who at seventy-two is in better shape than most women half her age, part of getting older has been learning to reconcile the dichotomy between how she feels and how she thought she would feel. "Just prior to my fiftieth birthday I was prepared to be depressed, really depressed. There was nothing obvious that was happening, but I braced myself for this imaginary punch, and then my kids threw me a surprise fiftieth birthday and it was wonderful. And that was the end of my depression.

"I think my fifties were the ten best years of my life. The kids were older and on their way, I was getting my Ph.D. in psychology, and I was into my analysis and feeling better about myself. I had finally worked out some of my personal difficulties." Ruth had always been extremely athletic, but her emotional well-being gave her an added boost. "I had a lot of energy. I was running and racing, and so I really felt good. I was doing things. I loved my new job. It was very exciting. Yeah, it was good. So really, the fifties were really great."

The momentum and feeling of possibility that Ruth discovered in her fifties and sixties has continued into her seventies, especially after she married Harry and jumped back into an intense sex life. "I'm really getting into things that will keep me vital and positive and interested and interesting. I'm still very intact physically. I don't feel old enough to have lost a lot, and I love that. I love to bike. I like to run. I like to do yoga." Ruth knows that she doesn't fit the model of the typical woman her age, but she says, "I don't know what it means to feel my age. I feel me. And I think that other people have a particular idea of what it's supposed to be like when you're in your seventies, and I clearly know that I don't fit that model. Generally speaking I don't want to comply with society's cultural idea that I'm not supposed to do something or be something or say something because I'm this age. *Uh-uh.*"

. . .

Marnie, seventy-five, a nationally ranked skier and aerobics teacher from Minnesota who has won gold medals and hopes to win one more, is another example of someone who has sustained her physical strength and agility. For Marnie competitive skiing inspires her to stay healthy and keeps her feeling young. "It is my passion. I mean, I just love it. I love the speed; I love the exhilaration. I love the fact that I'm on two racing teams and the average age of my pals is fifty. They're talking about their kids getting chicken pox; I'm talking about chicken pox but about my grandchildren."

People either react with amazement to Marnie's super-active lifestyle or think she's crazy. Either way they assume that her physical health and strength have come effortlessly, but this couldn't be further from the truth. Marnie has contended with ongoing physical and medical challenges. "People think I have it easy. I have had sixty-two surgical procedures, two babies by C-sections, a fake hip, a fake knee, a rod in my tibia, a fused right ankle, rotator cuff surgery. On and on and on. I had lung cancer for a week; they removed the bottom third of my right lung. So you don't go through all of those procedures and physical therapy postoperatively without looking after yourself."

When we asked Marnie what she thinks the secret to her physical resilience has been, she told us, "The fact that I absolutely look after my health. I pay very, very careful attention. I've taught aerobics since 1985. And I figure you only have one body; you jolly well better look after it. You better feed it and exercise. I have indeed a special diet, in that 90 percent of the time at every single meal I eat a protein, a vegetable, a fruit, and a starch. Even at breakfast. I took a grandson out to breakfast this morning. I had half a glass of orange juice, a single poached egg, a piece of dry toast, and half a cup of cooked vegetables. I'm pretty careful about butter. You do not compete nationally, let me tell you, in ski racing at altitudes without being in shape. I have a trainer and I pump iron three times a week, and I probably teach between four and five pool aerobics classes a week."

After a lifetime of intense physical training Marnie's not only in great physical shape, she actually feels stronger now than when she was younger, both physically and psychologically. "I was seventy-five on January 22. How my life is different is I have the confidence to do exactly what I want to do. And when you're younger, you do what your parents or other people want you to do." Of her future she says, "It doesn't have to look any different than it does now. I hope I'm still skiing. I know people who've skied into their nineties. I want to be one of them."

THE GRAYING OF THE GYM RAT

While a focus on exercise is less common among women born in the 1920s or 1930s, Maddie Dychtwald, sixty, who forecasts age trends, points out that it's very much part of the boomer mentality. "The boomer generation exercises more: I think twice as much as any other generation. It was the first generation of women to get out there and get involved in sports and fitness. They watched their parents age and turned around and said they didn't want to do it that way. Their parents and their grandparents grew old in a different time with a different set of values and priorities; they expected to grow old, and they accepted it more or less. The boomers don't have such a mellow attitude about aging.

"I think more and more women are [fighting aging], and I don't think it's in a superficial manner. I don't think wrinkles and gray hair is the modus operandi. It's more about keeping the energy and the vitality and the joie de vivre that we associate with youth. So they're really co-opting youth. They're taking the concept of youth, and they're bringing it with them into their middle and later years." Echoing Lauren Bacall's motto, "I'm not a has been, I'm a will be," more and more women are refusing to limit their options or range of activity because of age—no matter what society dictates.

LISTENING TO YOUR BODY

Betty says, "I am the only senior citizen I know who's not on any meds. My blood pressure goes up a little now and then—big fucking deal." Indeed, there's nothing in Betty's demeanor or her brisk gait that resembles those of an older person. Her secret is to be flexible, to keep listening to her body, and to do what makes her feel best. "So at forty I went vegetarian. No alcohol, and I was trying to come off cigarettes. I did smoke marijuana. That was kind of what was going on in the '70s. We were using marijuana as our fun drug, and we were eating vegetables and drinking apple juice and having a lot of sex. Then in my fifties I got kind of bored with the vegetables only, and I started eating more variety. By the time I hit my sixties, I thought, I want to have a glass of wine every now and then. So I started having wine with my meals. And meat, red meat. I really missed red meat.

I'm a carnivore, there's no doubt about it. But I pace it, you know. Red meat once every week, two weeks. We go down to the farmer's market. We get organic meat, organic chicken, organic food. We clean our water. I don't drink water out of the tap. I don't do sodas anymore. I take a Perrier and put a little fresh fruit juice in it. I try to hold it down to one glass of wine, two maximum."

As a sex expert, Betty sees some women who aren't taking very good care of themselves, and she says there's no question it affects them sexually. "If we ignore our bodies, we do not have a relationship with our bodies. If we don't start looking at what we're putting in this end and what's coming out that end, forget sex." Watching her own mother age informed Betty about how she wanted to do it differently. "I remember when I used to go up and visit my mom, I'd say, 'Bessie, come on, get down here on the floor with me.' And then I'd give her a massage. And the best place was to do it on the floor because I could move around her. And she said the reason she didn't want to get on the floor was she was afraid she couldn't get up. I mean, she had a fat butt. She was small on the top and big at the butt. So I showed her how you can roll over on your side and then push yourself up, one leg at a time. Because that's the fear that [older people have], that they can't get up. So I have been going to my gym on a regular basis. I use my ball. I stretch. And I started meditating at the first of the year. If older people would just get down on the floor and stretch they'd feel a helluva lot better."

NECESSARY REPAIRS

Of course, the body does break down with age, most notably the joints. Of the women we interviewed, many had
had knee or hip replacement. While some, like Betty, worried
about the overprescription of pharmaceuticals, all hailed joint
replacement as a godsend.

In Betty's case, her hip pain increased gradually over time,
so that she didn't immediately realize the severity of the problem. By the time she did, she felt physically debilitated, which
made dealing with the situation more challenging. "The body
I had most of my life got taken away from me. It started happening in the early part of my sixties, and it was like, Oh, so this
is what old age is! I can see if there wasn't a cure for this, if
there wasn't a surgery, I'd be sitting in a wheelchair right now. I
don't know if I'd still be around. I think that's when people just
take off.

"The scariest time was the few years leading up to the surgery,
where I was losing my mobility. I was in my early sixties, between
sixty-one and sixty-two, and when I finally did the surgeries I
was sixty-seven. I was terrified. I'd never done doctors. I'd never
had a sick day in my life. It wasn't my MO. And all of a sudden
every step was agony. And then it would clear up, and it was like
everything was okay again. And then something would happen
where it would start in again. I tried all of the alternative healing
systems. And finally I was at the point where it was either sit
down and shut up or get a hip replacement, because I'd tried
everything else. They say when the pain is bad enough you'll go

for anything. So I waited until the pain was bad enough. I mean, I was at the stage where anything, anything would help. It had gotten to that point."

Even after deciding to have the procedure, it took a lot of emotional preparation for Betty to feel comfortable with the idea of surgery. "I had to go to a therapist to deal with my fear of surgery. I used a hypnotic technique that the therapist teaches people. And I also watched the operation performed on television. In other words, I informed myself with everything that was going to happen. Then I started to work with my body by having conversations with it several times a day about what was going to happen: 'Don't panic, body, because this is something that's going to help and make us feel better.' And then I would say, 'After the surgery there will be no infections, there will be no complications, my blood pressure will return to normal, the wound will begin to heal immediately, and I will feel no more pain.' It's called positive thinking; it's no mystery.

"I healed very rapidly. It's three months of prefocused physical therapy. And afterwards, I was a born-again hedonist. It's like you're new! You're renewed! And the biggest thing that happened was right away, people would look at me, and they'd say, 'You look so different.' And then I'd say, 'Yeah because I'm not in pain,' because pain causes your face to contract. And the pain was gone. To live pain free . . . it was like [takes deep breath] . . . whew!"

Reflecting on her operation, she says, "It's a miracle operation. In retrospect, I think I would've done it sooner. I wouldn't have waited so long. I did a lot of research. I don't just go blindly into the night, so I also wanted to talk to some of my doctor's patients. They'll give you names of people to talk to. I'm also on

that list. I've had women call me. Absolutely, I say. Do not hesi-
tate. It's safe; it's totally successful. It's one of the few things that
I can say that I admire the medical professionals for. They're
good carpenters. They know how to put the screws in and put the
body back together. When it comes to food and nutrition and
internal organs and the spinal column and sex, they don't know
from shit. But screwing a body back together, like building a
piece of furniture, they're the best."

Even after the surgery it took Betty time to heal completely
and regain full use of her body. "I didn't get furniture until after
the surgery because I couldn't bend. You can't bend your hips at
a ninety-degree angle. You have to wait for it to settle in, build the
muscle and the tendons back." Having sex again also took time.
"I couldn't get my legs apart! Visualize bone on bone. The carti-
lage was worn out. It was just this grinding bone pain. It's deep,
deep pain." But ultimately the hip replacement allowed Betty to
continue enjoying the full lifestyle that she had before and to start
one of the wildest sexual escapades of her life at sixty-nine with
Erik, twenty-two.

After Freddie had her knee replacement in her early seventies,
she was able to walk better than she had a decade earlier. Was she
afraid? Yes, that's why she had them both done at the same time.
"I knew if I had one done I'd never go back. There was pain, and
I had to go through a lot of rehabilitation, but it was more than
worth it." And for Marnie, knee- and hip-replacement surgery
have meant not only walking better but the ongoing rush of being
able to ski down a mountain past people half her age.

OUR EVOLVING RELATIONSHIP WITH OUR BODIES

While all the women we talked to struggled with the reality that their bodies were aging, they had drastically different opinions about whether or not plastic surgery was a solution. Some adamantly opposed it; others felt it was the right choice. In general there is the assumption that a woman's relationship with her body will get worse with age. But like all relationships, there are good times and bad, and it has the potential to get better.

Harriet describes how age and experience have actually helped her to feel better about her body, even though it's less classically perfect than it was when she was a renowned young beauty. "I'm not the kind of woman who's going to have a face-lift and a boob implantation. That's not me, and I will never do that. Still, I think my relationship with my body has become more loving. It's strange, because I've had several bodies, as we all have. When I was a kid I was very, very flat chested. I had no hips,

According to AARP's study "Lifestyles, Dating and Romance: A Study of Midlife Singles," only 24 percent rate "staying young looking" as important to them. Compare that to the 62 percent who give high marks to "a fulfilling relationship," 55 percent who rate "feeling good about myself" highly, and 53 percent who emphasize the importance of "staying healthy and physically fit."

which I still don't have. I had no butt, really. And I was very slim and skinny and lanky, which apparently appealed to certain kinds of people, but I didn't like it very much. Then, when I had my son, I developed tits. I loved them, and I still love them. They are not as pretty as they used to be, and they kind of droop a little, which is inevitable. But I love my body. I stroke my body. I love my body. I'm moved by my body. I have this scar on my knee now [from knee replacement] and I stroke it. . . . Y'know, I feel it's the only body I'm ever going to have [*laughs*]. I feel that I look good. In the summer I wear a bikini. Most women my age don't. And I've got a big belly, so it's not exactly aesthetically pleasing. But I like it. I feel good in a bikini. I feel good nude. I guess I've always been an exhibitionist. I've always loved the nude beach. I don't know why."

On the other hand, Freddie told us that after looking in the mirror and feeling uncomfortable with the way she looked for several years, she decided to have a face-lift to change some minor details on her neck, and was totally pleased with the results. "I chose to have plastic surgery a decade ago not so much because of the wrinkles but because there were parts of my neck I had not liked for many years, and so I saw no reason not to get rid of them if it was possible. That didn't have a whole lot to do with what soci-

The percentage of women sixty-five+ undertaking plastic surgery remains very low (less than 4 percent, reports a 2001 AARP study). In fact, the same study shows that more than 90 percent of those surveyed are satisfied with the way they look for their age, and 60 percent feel that inner beauty is more important than physical appearance.

ety said, but I didn't like them. After the plastic surgery I felt very good that I did it. I've never had a desire to do it again, because what I wanted to accomplish, I accomplished. And it hasn't really gone back. There are more wrinkles now, but that isn't what bothers me. I don't mind the wrinkles."

Betty also decided to have plastic surgery and was surprised at how well it turned out. "I decided, all right. I thought I would never do cosmetic surgery—never, never, never. It's vanity. It's stupid. I'm not going to play into it . . . and then I thought, Get over yourself. It's so commonplace, you have the money, you have a younger lover. Why not? So I interviewed different doctors and I found one that I really liked, and she said, 'I'm not going to do anything extreme. I'm not going to do anything extravagant, so people won't know that you've had cosmetic surgery; they'll just think that you look rested.' And that's how it turned out. I'm amazed, y'know. It's me. It's not someone else's face. People see me and they say, 'Oh, have you lost weight? You look really . . . Oh, you're in love!'"

Joani, seventy, had a breast reduction about twenty years ago and a tummy tuck about twelve years ago, and both made her feel better about herself. She says, "Especially after the breast reduction, I felt more sexually attractive than before. I used to be very uncomfortable and embarrassed, and I couldn't wear shirts that buttoned in the front. I'm quite short waisted and I'm only five foot two, so having big breasts was really hard, especially when I was a teenager and young adult. The scars from the surgeries really don't bother me. By the time a lover sees my body without clothing he's not going to care, so I don't either." These surgeries have made Joani feel better about her body now, at seventy, than she did in her twenties, thirties, or forties.

HORMONE REPLACEMENT

Along with skin and bones, the body changes hormonally, which affects women in very different ways. Some feel hornier than ever, and others are less inclined to want sex. For women who experience a difficult menopause, there is the option of hormone replacement therapy, a highly controversial topic not only in the media but also among the women we talked to. While many enjoyed the benefits of hormone replacement in their fifties and sixties (enjoying continued vaginal wetness and elastic skin), most have gone off it in the last few years because of the recent studies linking its use to an increased risk of cancer.

Ellen, seventy-four, was on hormone replacement during menopause and says now, "I wouldn't say that I felt one way or another about [menopause, but] when I went off [of hormone replacement therapy] a couple years ago because they were concerned about it causing cancer, within a few months I began to see the changes. I feel like I'm going through more of a menopause now than I did in my late fifties or early sixties. I'm much dryer than I ever was in my life, all parts of me, including my skin and internal secretions. Absolutely dryer. And less desire. And was it Maya Angelou who said that as she ages she thinks there is a great race between her breasts to reach her waist? I'm seeing that happen. I've seen an enormous amount of change. I was at the doctor yesterday, and I lost half an inch in a year of my total height. There may be inaccuracies, but I've seen that I keep on measuring smaller and smaller, and I wasn't tall to start off with. It's interesting because I feel like I'm going through menopause now, at seventy-four." If it weren't for the dangerous side effects, Ellen says she would definitely still be on hormone replacement therapy. "There's been a temptation, but I don't think I would tempt other forms of sickness by that."

When we asked Cornell University gynecologist Peggy Polaneczky if she thought the Women's Health Initiative studies reported in the *Journal of the American Medical Association* linking hormone replacement therapy and cancer were accurate she told us, "I think the studies did what they were designed to do. They were accurate in that they answered the question, Should every woman take hormone replacement? and the answer to that is: The risks outweigh the benefits. The study was not meant to ask the question, Should women who have hot flashes or symptoms of menopause use hormone replacement? The study was designed to ask, Should every woman take hormone replacement? And that answer is no, at least in this point and time. The problem is that that data has been extrapolated to mean no one should ever take it for any reason, and that is where the inaccuracy is coming in. These studies are being used to deny women access to a legitimate medication that has benefits as well as risks, like any medication out there, including aspirin, which might be appropriate for certain women with certain conditions."

C. Noel Bairey Merz, M.D., holder of the Women's Guild Chair in Women's Health and medical director of Women's

Health at Cedars-Sinai, was quoted in the *Science Daily News* as saying, "While it is certainly significant when a major national clinical trial is stopped, it's important to understand that the actual increased risk for any of these conditions was very small (1.4 percent), and the breast cancer risk occurred only in women who were on the therapy for five years." She also said, "The death rate did not increase at all," adding that the estrogen-only component of the trial was still ongoing.

The study indicated that for every ten thousand women taking combined HRT each year, there would be seven more heart attacks, eight excess breast cancers, and eight more strokes than would have occurred had the drugs not been taken. We asked Dr. Polaneczky if she still feels comfortable suggesting hormone replacement therapy to a woman suffering from symptoms of menopause. "Yes," she replied, "that's definitely one of the treatment options that they can consider if they are willing to accept the risks, which according to the Women's Health Initiative we would define as increased risk of breast cancer, heart disease, and stroke. These are not high risks, but they are real, and women must accept them if they are going to get the benefits, and depending on the woman, her decision to use or not to use will depend on how that risk-benefit balance works for her."

Dr. Bairey Merz echoed the idea of trade-offs: "The study has shown a strong reduction in hip fractures for women on HRT, which means that women with a family history of osteoporosis or brittle bones might want to consider continuing the therapy. However, it is very important that they undergo mammograms annually to screen for breast cancer," she emphasized

For women who just don't want to assume the risks, Dr. Polaneczky told us, "Oh well, there's other medications they can use. We don't just say here's hormone replacement, and they say no, we say here are the options to treat the conditions that you have. You can take hormone replacement. We can also try a low dose of an antidepressant like Paxil, Prozac, Zoloft, or Effexor, or a drug called Neurontin, which is an antiseizure drug. These have been studied in small trials, but they have been shown to be about 65 percent as effective as estrogen. They will reduce hot flashes by about 65 percent, so they're an option. And then there are nonmedical things they can do, like they can avoid things that trigger hot flashes, such as drinking wine or caffeine. You change temperature, so women can make sure they dress in layers of clothing and avoid stress. There are a lot of nonmedical things that can help. And then if vaginal dryness is the only problem, most women can safely use vaginal estrogen, in my opinion."

Whereas Betty has had plastic surgery and hip replacement, she's always drawn the line at hormone replacement therapy. She says she would never even consider it. "Never, never, never. All you have to do is read some of the side effects. My God, it's four pages of small type; you have to get out a magnifying glass. Ridiculous."

Several years ago, however, Betty began taking natural, bio-identical hormones. She told us how she found out about them. "I had now gotten into my sixties, I was having some pain during penetration, and I was trying to figure it out. So, I went to the doctor and got a bone scan, and she examined my vagina and said, 'Yes, it's definitely thinned out. Why don't you take some of these natural hormones, Betty? In case you want to have partner sex." I said, 'I'm not going to take hormones with all that.' But

she said, 'These are natural.' And she was one of the top endo-
crinologists in Santa Barbara, and she was a woman, and she
was hip, and I just trusted her. And I said, 'Oh, really. I didn't
know that.' She said, 'Well, it's relatively new. They're certainly
not advertising it. The pharmaceutical companies will see to it.
They're trying to get rid of them now.

"So I started taking them. They're made from soybean plants.
And they are bioidentical. My body goes, 'Oh, yeah, this is what
we used to have.' Slurp. Take it and use it. And I had the opportunity of going through a small portion of what a transsexual
from male to female would go through as I started taking the
female hormones. All of a sudden it's like, my breasts are tender
again, and I'm sort of like going through a period, a cycle. I actually had a breakthrough period. And it's like, oh! I'm sixty-five
now, sixty-four, and I'm thinking, God, I wouldn't mind having
a baby. Wouldn't that be fabulous? Never had that feeling before
in my life. And I start looking at guys, saying '*Ooh*, I'd like to
fuck him. . . .' So hormones, *whoa-ho-ho*, did they play a major
role. I had no idea."

We loved the idea of natural hormones and found out after film
festival screenings of our documentary *Still Doing It* that some of
the women who heard Betty rave about them immediately went
out to buy them. So we decided to ask Dr. Polaneczky what she
thought about bioidentical hormones. She told us, "Well, they
work. They're estrogen, and they work just as well as the synthet-
ics, but women have to assume that they have the same risks. You
can talk to any doctor, and they will tell you this; I'm not unusual
in this respect. The only people that are telling otherwise are

these non-M.D.s and pharmacists and people that are making huge amounts of money pushing bioidenticals. I had one woman who went out to some website in California, stopped her hormone replacement, came to me, and said, 'You know, I'm not taking those horrible drugs that you gave me. Here's what I'm taking.' And what she was taking was the exact same thing I had given her at three times the dose. What I was giving her happened to have a pharmaceutical brand name on it, but what I was giving her was bioidentical estrogen, bioidentical progesterone, and she was now taking three times that dose compounded by some pharmacy out in California and said to me, 'I'm not taking a breast cancer risk, and that's why I'm taking this.' So, huge, huge misunderstanding. There's a really nice book called *Is It Hot in Here? Or Is It Just Me?* by Barbara Kantrowitz and Pat Wingert Kelly. I think it's the best one out there, and they've got a good section on bioidenticals there."

Clearly the use of pharmaceutical hormone replacement or bioidentical hormones has a profound and positive effect on women's skin, vaginal dryness, bone density, and in some cases sexual desire, but it's complicated. As we age, we will all have to stay on top of the onslaught of conflicting information and decide what's best. Taking care of our aging bodies is clearly a huge responsibility. There are important and complicated decisions that in the end no one else can make for us.

HONORING THE AGING BODY

Meryl Streep describes her relationship with aging as a process of acceptance and self-empowerment. She says,

"I like who I am now. Other people may not. I'm comfortable. I feel freer now. I don't want growing older to matter to me." Frances, eighty-six, says, "My body is my body. That's the state of my grace. I can't be sorry because my arms are flabby or my belly is flabby. That's what it is. You live with what you got."

For Lainie, sixty-six, a sensuous beauty who has devoted her life to singing, it's not just living with what you've got, it's really loving and enjoying what you've got. She says, "I believe that I'm going to live to be a very old lady. That's my agreement with the universe. I'm going to be an old lady, and my intention is to be as healthy and as beautiful and as sexy as I can be until the day I die. And so I get the exercise that I need. I take good care of myself. I want to look in the mirror and say, 'You look good. All right. You look pretty.' I want to be pretty forever. I really do. My relationship with myself and my body is that I have to look in the mirror and still say, 'I'm a pretty girl.'"

For many of the women we spoke to, aging brings not only aches and pains but also a deep respect for the physical body they've lived with for so long. Despite knee surgery and having to walk with a cane, Harriet says, "I think I love my body more now than I ever did."

8.

DEALING WITH LOSS:
THE JOURNEY CONTINUES

No matter what you do, age brings losses. For those of us lucky enough to live a long life, there's no question we're going to have to deal with some. It might be the death of someone we love. Or health problems. Or it might be a more abstract sensation. Life involves so many dramatic changes that over time it can feel like we are losing aspects of ourselves.

When we started interviewing women for our documentary film *Still Doing It*, our focus was on older women's relationships and sexuality. But right away we were struck by both the losses older women were dealing with and the fearless attitude that so

AARP's 2003 study, "Lifestyles, Dating and Romance: A Study of Midlife Singles," revealed that women age sixty and older tended to have a more optimistic outlook than younger women did. And these women were far more sanguine about their prospects than middle-aged men. Among adults age forty-five and up, nonpartnered men age forty-five to forty-nine tend to have the least-positive outlook on life.

many had in terms of coping with them. Despite hardships they seemed to feel more celebratory about life than most younger people do. As Harriet told us, "being closer to the end than the beginning certainly has an impact on the way you feel about things. I mean, I just value every joy that I can taste so much more. When you're young you take so much for granted."

MOURNING YOUTH:
HARRIET CONFRONTS HER AGE

We met Harriet after putting an ad in New York's *Village Voice* that announced we were looking for women who would be willing to participate in our documentary film. The ad called for women over sixty-five who "still felt sexual, whether they were in a relationship or not." Harriet responded to our ad immediately, telling us it was an offer she couldn't refuse. "You never see someone asking for sexual older women," she said with a laugh. And once she was given the opportunity to talk about her sexuality, Harriet had a lot to tell.

For Harriet, a bohemian, sex has always been a huge part of her identity. In her fifties, Harriet started not one, but two relationships with men fifteen and twenty years younger than she. By the time we first interviewed her at seventy-three, however, these relationships had lost their steam: One had ended after a decade, and the other had become less than satisfying because of her lover's inability to "get it up." But ever the optimist, Harriet was looking for a relationship (or two) and was totally unabashed about her predilection for handsome young men.

One day during the production of the documentary, Harriet

became curious about how she looked on videotape. We warned her that in comparison with the soft focus and lighting of Holly-wood movies, our low-budget film didn't glamorize the women being interviewed. Harriet still insisted that she wanted to "see herself." And when she did, it was a starkly real vision. Though still charismatic and compelling, with a fabulous mane of long hair, Harriet, suddenly for the first time, came face-to-face with how she truly looks, as opposed to the younger version that she imagined. And she found it painful to see that she is, in fact, an older woman. She told us, "After seeing your film and seeing how old I really look—which I really wasn't totally cognizant of—if I'm lucky enough to get another lover I don't know how I'm going to feel now, because I'm really over the hill, honey. I'm really beginning to feel that. I'm feeling pretty like I'm past it, you know? And that's terrible, especially since I do have this pen-chant for younger guys. I would feel bereaved if I never . . . but I see how I looked in the film. I look pretty old. Somehow I hadn't acknowledged that."

Questioning her attractiveness and sex appeal at seventy-three was a difficult process for Harriet, who has been regarded as a great beauty for most of her life. An artist's model, teacher, and writer, she was sought after by a host of male and female art-ists and intellectuals (including the late Susan Sontag), both in the United States and in Paris, where she lived for many years. Being recognized as a beauty had become an integral part of her identity and vital to her self-worth. "It was always very impor-tant for me to be seen as beautiful. I guess I needed the reassur-ance or something."

Before showing her the footage we had feared that Harriet would drop out of the project if she wasn't happy with the way she looked on camera. But Harriet had only wanted the chance to "see herself," not to back out of an exploration of her life. A few weeks later, she told us, "A lot of what I'm writing now has to do with age. I'm mourning . . . I'm mourning my youth."

NO LIMIT

At eighty-six, Frances seemed to have already dealt with her share of loss in life: a divorce from her first husband in her early sixties, the death of two subsequent lovers, the death of her son, and the gradual loss of her eyesight. But amazingly none of this had weakened her spirit or quelled her passion for life. When we met her, she was still maintaining a sexual relationship with David, her lover of six years, despite having had to move to a nursing home four years earlier.

The first time we went to San Francisco to interview her about her life and her partnership with David, we were instantly struck by the vibe between them. Being in the room with them it was easy to forget that you were in a nursing home because the energy between them was electric. But physically, David had aged far better than Frances. At eighty-eight he was strong, with an energetic stride and upright posture. He seemed capable of taking care of himself and Frances. It was touching to see how he responded to Frances in such a powerful sexual way and also lovingly pushed her in her wheelchair when she got tired from walking.

So, it was both surprising and poignant when Frances called one day to tell us that David had died suddenly. When we returned to San Francisco a few weeks later, she told us how unexpected his death had been. But the last time they spoke to each other, Frances sensed something in the tone of his voice, and even before she realized he had died she felt devastated. "David called to say good morning. He said good morning in a voice that I didn't recognize as David's, and I cried all day. I cried all day not yet knowing that he had died."

David had been healthy until the day he died. Frances never thought about the possibility of his dying suddenly. "We said about dying we're going out together. He said, 'Yes we will, we'll go out together.' But we didn't go out together. And it was very, very hard. Those first few weeks were terribly hard." Frances felt that if she continued to allow herself to miss David, the feeling of loss would destroy her. When we asked her if she missed his physical touch, she immediately replied, "I don't. I don't miss the physical part. If I began to miss the physical part of it, I would go mad. You use what you have and go forward with what you have. I have no way else of describing it."

David's death brought Frances's own existential situation into sharp focus. "He was the great love of my life, but I don't believe in heaven, and I don't believe that we'll be joined again. David and I often said that religious people are lucky because they have something to hang on to. But as irreligious people, we know all we have to hang on to is ourselves, and hanging on to yourself is pretty darn hard."

THE LONG GOOD-BYE

Like Frances, Marnie, seventy-five, also had to deal with the death of her partner. But unlike David's sudden death,

Marnie's husband, Carl, died slowly. While the gradual decline of her husband's health gave Marnie time to prepare for his death, it also completely changed the dynamic of their relationship as Marnie became her husband's caretaker.

"At the end he couldn't do the bathroom drill himself. That is very tough for a man who'd owned his own business and was a leader in the community. My choice always was, do I take Carl into the men's room, which is embarrassing for me, or do I bring him into the ladies' room on the premise that more ladies are going to understand what you're doing? And nine times out of ten I took him into the ladies' room. It was interesting because I just took two grandchildren to the children's museum this past week, because they were on spring vacation, and I saw the door of that ladies' room and it just brought back that very uncomfortable memory. And I'm sure it was just as tough on him.

"The best probable thing happened in the last year of our marriage. I don't think a whole lot of couples have this opportunity. I would say Carl wasn't quite as spiritual perhaps as I was, and I felt tremendously strongly that he have enough faith not to be frightened when he died. So, in the last year of his life, even though mentally he wasn't at top drawer, every couple of days I'd read him a couple of pages from *The Purpose-Driven Life* and then would talk about it. And I said to him once, 'I'm going to die, you're going to die, we all do, flowers die, whatever—is there anything of which you're going to be afraid?' And he said, 'Yes.' And I said, 'What is that?' And he said, 'Leaving you,' which was so sweet. And I spent the next couple of months explaining to him it would be very, very tough for me but I would be okay. I have many, many friends, fabulous family. I would be okay and for him not to worry about that. And, honestly, when Carl did die I was very sanguine that he was calm and felt that he was going on to a better place. That had been my goal, and I don't think too many couples have the opportunity to talk about death while one of them is dying. Maybe they do. I've never found anybody else who has had the experience that I had with Carl. And even though his death was perfectly ghastly I think it's a huge gift that we were given that time to have those conversations."

After Carl's death, Marnie was instantly reminded that life doesn't stand still and that there is no limit on pain. "A week after Carl died I chose to have a knee replaced. Well, that wasn't a very smart choice because I'd looked after Carl for five years and my immune system was very, very weakened, and as a result of that I got an infection in that knee and had six subsequent procedures on that knee. One month later they discovered lung cancer at the Mayo Clinic, and they removed the bottom lobe of my right lung. All of this was because of my immune system, because I'm the hugest believer in you cannot control what your feelings do to your body. And after forty-four years of a wonderful marriage, to see your husband slowly die and then have him die got to me obviously, and it got to me in a very physical way. So, recouping from that was the toughest recouping that I had to do. But even harder for me was getting back into ski racing again because I had to overcome the fear of what it would be like racing on a fused ankle, on a fake knee. And it took me all last winter—it took me six clinics once a week. I didn't start in the starting gate. I skied outside the course until the very last gate from the bottom. So I skied in one gate through the finish line. Next time maybe I went up and skied two gates from the bottom. And it took me six weeks to go up and up and up and start in the start house and ski the entire course and go through the finish line."

Marnie knew skiing was a life force, and in having the courage to go back to it, despite her emotional and physical frailties, she gave herself the will to truly live again.

THE SHRINKING CIRCLE

The reality of living a long life is that you risk losing not only your lovers but also your close friends. Three years after the death of her best friend from college, Freddie is still grieving and fears that there are intimate parts of herself that she may never be able to share again. For Ellen, seventy-four, whose lesbian circle has been an alternative family for her since she came out in the 1970s, the loss of friends has been particularly difficult. She says, "I know that life is very tenuous because I have lost many of my close friends. I have lost my relatives. [And because of that] I have in a way lost parts of myself."

But that loss has also increased the intensity with which Ellen savors her current relationship. "When I met Dolores at sixty-seven, I was very much aware that there wasn't that much time left, that maybe at most I had ten good years, twenty good years if I really pushed the envelope. I'm only learning what I am through the process of living, and the extreme awareness of connecting physically is an echo of being alive. And while you touch and while you are close to someone else and while you are sexual you are not alone. And the ultimate fear, I think, from the day we're born to the day we die, is being alone. For me it's very much a constant sense of urgency to make this work, to savor it as I did not when I was younger, because younger life is something that you can use up and throw away. When you're in your seventies you know there's not an endless supply of your breath and your years."

LIVING WITH CANCER

Many of the women we spoke to had lived through early stages of cancer. In cases like Marnie's, it was quickly diagnosed and treated, and didn't affect her life for long. But other women we interviewed, who had later stages of cancer, had to deal with far more arduous treatments as well as their own mortality.

Elaine, eighty, says, "In the last five years I've had cancer twice: surgery, chemo, radiation. I had colon cancer, and then, two years after that, I had breast cancer. Two thousand four was the year from hell; I had a partial mastectomy. I had a wonderful physician. She said, 'We try not to take the whole breast, but I will tell you, I was shocked at how many lymph nodes you had that were cancerous.' Out of twenty-one, she took eighteen. But I trust her.

"With the chemo I lost my appetite. I lost twenty pounds. When the treatments were finished I went on to radiation, which lasts thirty days. I got a little burnt, so they sent me to a dermatologist. It's all healed up. They sent me to physical therapy so that I would not lose the range of motion in that arm. They've taken fantastic care of me. It's amazing. Whatever my doctors say, I just feel that they know best. We have wonderful comprehensive cancer care here. You know how frightened you are, never knowing what to expect. And then my blood count went down so low it was dangerous, so they had to stop the chemo, and I had to have blood transfusions. I'll tell you, 2004, I wouldn't want to live through that again, but I survived. I'm a survivor of two and a half years. And I feel good, so it was well worth it."

Elaine uses every occasion she gets to celebrate life. "We celebrate every birthday [in our family]. It's a blessing. I think people fear old age because of their mortality. I think most people my age think this is the end of the line, and they think about death. To me it's just wasted energy. There are just some things we can't do anything about, and if you accept them life is a lot easier. I just had the big eight-oh. I never would have thought; I don't feel eighty. In a sense, when I see other people and hear their complaints, I think, God! I must be in pretty good shape! I don't have many aches and pains or any replaced joints. Maybe I'm sexual because I have everything I was born with. I never had a hysterectomy or anything like that. I went on a cruise for my birthday, took ten family members and friends. We just had a ball. It was wonderful."

Like Elaine, Carmen, sixty-four, was also diagnosed with advanced cancer. We met her a year after her treatments but didn't know that she had been sick. When she greeted us at the door her short hair (only recently grown back after falling out) elegantly heightened the beauty of her angular face. But the truth is, Carmen was just coming out of a long physical ordeal. After monitoring the lump on her lung for a year, X-rays showed that the cancer was spreading. Yet, listening to Carmen tell the story of her ongoing treatment, we were struck by her incredibly upbeat attitude. "I remember I was at the doctor's office, and the doctor told me what was going to happen, so I had to call my son and tell him that the doctor was going to have to have a meeting with my family to tell them what was going on. Everybody was, like, 'You lied to us. You never told us.' I said, 'Well, listen, I wanted to know myself what was really going on before I involved the whole family.' "

Carmen remembers that after the family meeting with her doctor, she instantly felt an urge to get on with her life. "We all walked downstairs, and my family was, like, 'Well, are you going home?' I said, 'No, I'm going to work!' My children said, 'You are such a weird woman. How are you gonna go to work?' I said, 'What do you want me to do?' I left the doctor's office, and I got on the bus, and I went to work." Carmen had a similar surprise for the people at work, where she announced to everyone that she was going on vacation. She remembers, "I had two jobs, and I said, 'I'm not coming in tomorrow . . . I'm going on vacation! I'll come back in three weeks.' So at ten o'clock I came home, and we went on vacation. We went to the Poconos for two weeks. Oh, I had a ball! I went water rafting. I went fishing, because I love fishing. You know, I did all that stuff for two weeks, and then I came back, had my operation, and then I had my chemo for four months. I'm still going through it, you know. . . ."

Staying positive and letting go of fear are skills Carmen claims she has honed. "You enjoy life more when you're older and you're not scared. You know, you're not scared of anything. I guess when I was faced with the cancer, it was, like, 'Oh well, this is another tribulation in my life, and I'm just gonna see what happens. I just went through with the operation. I was twenty-six days in the hospital. When I left there, I had all my hair, but when I came home . . . four months later I lost it. I remember I was going to

church, and my granddaughter was here with me—she's eight—
and I was in the bathroom, and I went to put the comb in my hair
and my hair came out. And she calls me, she says, 'Nonny, your
hair's falling out!' I had already explained to her about the cancer
and the chemo and what was going to happen, so to her it was,
like, 'Your hair's falling out! What are we going to do?' I said,
'I'm going to put a scarf on.' So I put a scarf on my hair, and we
went to church. Everybody asks me, How do you feel about that?
And I say, I don't know; it's just something that happened,
and I dealt with it, and here I am, and I will move forward and
move on."

Carmen's effervescent love of life seems to constantly infuse
her with energy and enthusiasm, even while dealing with the
harsh physical side effects of chemotherapy. Although her cancer
treatment has taken years, Carmen feels that she's held on to the
things that she loves most about life. "You don't get cured within
a year or two, because your hair falls off—now my hair's growing
back—and my appetite is not the same. Everything is different.
It's like your whole body changes, and the way you're thinking,
and you want to do more. . . . But I still go out because I love
dancing. That's one of my best things. I love the movies; I love the
theater; I like parties; I like to entertain. . . . I still do most of
the things I did before I got cancer. Nothing tells you to stop living. I mean, if you're a survivor you just go forward and do more
things than you did before. Last year I went to Florida, and in
August, praise God, I want to go to Puerto Rico. You know? It
doesn't stop you from doing a lot of things.

"But I do see the world so differently, with the cancer I went
through. I respect it, and I appreciate it more that I'm going to be

sixty-five and I'm still here. And I know that I'm going to live longer. And I'm going to enjoy more. I still like to get dressed up and look pretty. And I'm planning a big sixty-fifth birthday party to celebrate that I'm still here."

Elaine, too, has maintained her appetite for life despite the fact that there's a high risk her cancer will recur. "They got all of the cancer in the surgery for the colon cancer, but they weren't that sure of the breast cancer because of all the lymph nodes they found that were cancerous, and they tell me there's a high risk of the cancer recurring. I just lost a friend last week. She had been cancer free for a few years, and then all of a sudden it popped up again and she's gone." But rather than live in a perpetual state of fear Elaine is working for the American Cancer Society, helping to increase cancer awareness in the African-American community, a group in which there is not enough early detection of the disease.

"I'm giving back, because I'm a volunteer for the American Cancer Society. I was chosen by them to be an ambassador representing the state of Rhode Island in Washington, D.C., and I went! I was there September 19–21, and I sat down with congressmen because we want increased funding for research, for treatment. This cancer's running amok, my God! People who don't have insurance should not be denied mammograms. The American Cancer Society is offering screenings for nothing, but people think that because they don't have coverage, they aren't eligible. My picture and story were chosen to be one of the months for our most recent calendar. All the women pictured are cancer survivors and women of color. The calendar is to make women of color aware that there are resources available to them. I meet women of color who are forty-five who have never had a mammogram or a Pap smear. Oh, my God, you can't do that! We were trying to raise awareness in D.C."

Elaine's advocacy work reminds her how lucky she is to still be alive and vibrant. "It is meaningful because I survived. For two and a half years, I'm cancer free. And I need to give back. This is my way of saying thank you, thank you. Let me see if I can help someone. We have a program called Reach to Recovery. This is all about doctors referring their new cancer patients to us so that we can, in some way, encourage and help a new cancer person hold on because having cancer doesn't always have to mean a death sentence."

Elaine feels it is critical to remind women of color to take care of themselves. "We're so busy nurturing our families and husbands that we forget about ourselves. I don't think some women are getting the tests they need because of that. Some think they're not eligible because they don't have a certain kind of HMO. This is a dreadful disease, and everyone you know is connected to someone who has it. It is helpful when another black lady can look at me and say, 'Wow! How did you do it?' And I can sit down and say to her, 'It can be done!' "

Elaine says, "I have a lot of faith. I believe in God. I believe that there's some things in our lives that we can't deal with, so we have to turn to him. Ultimately, His will will be done. I think my attitude, my love for life, and my love for people has gotten me through. I've always had this positive attitude, even as a kid. Maybe it has something to do with being an only child and wanting to be accepted by people. Maybe that's what it's all about. I think my attitude about life . . . a lot of people don't have it. I live in a senior complex right now, and three quarters of these people feel that this is the end of the line and what is there left for me to do? And I'm thinking, Oh, my God! How come I don't feel like that?"

Certainly there are a multitude of ways to deal with and make sense of loss, and infuse greater meaning into life. Carmen's struggle with cancer is a constant reminder to appreciate every moment. Elaine has used it as an entry into a whole new life. Marnie has used her struggle with the loss of her husband and her subsequent bout with cancer and knee surgery as inspiration to push herself physically and ski at a higher level than ever before, which was not easy. "I don't care if you're an Olympic-caliber racer, no matter what your level there is going to be fear. To me the biggest challenge of my life has been overcoming those fears and going back and racing after I had all these medical procedures." When we asked Marnie what fueled her ambition to meet that challenge, she told us, "Energy and passion, because I want to do it. I won a gold medal nationally three years ago in a different age group. This coming winter, I will be in the seventy-five to eighty-year-old category. I'm going to try, I'm going to give it one more go to see if I can win another gold medal nationally." Even though many of her close friends think she's crazy, the rush of skiing and the intense training necessary to prepare to race is what keeps Marnie feeling like she's got her finger on the pulse of life.

MAKING SENSE OF CHANGE

While loss and change are obviously difficult, many women like Harriet feel that grappling with aging has clarified their priorities. "Figure I have ten years of keeping my marbles, being able to move at all, being sort of acceptable. There are certain hang-ups that I don't want to deal with anymore: nostalgia or regret. I think somehow my ego has reached a level that it never had before. I'm very sort of proud of myself lately. I don't know why but truly, partly intellectually. It's like my mind is doing good work. You know, my body's coming apart. It's as though I'm functioning intellectually better than I ever did in my whole life, and my writing is better."

Much of Harriet's writing now is about sex and aging. In an excerpt she read us from her story "The Starman," her reverence and craving for sex is conveyed against the backdrop of the bay beach where she vacations every summer.

A falling star shoots across the black velvet sky and plunges into the water. Suddenly a tall, slim shadow appears out of the shimmering bay and walks straight up the beach toward me. We are both naked, hidden by the dark. He reaches one long, smooth arm across the chair and rests it on my thighs. I open them slightly. The odors of the fishy bay, the grass, our skins blend in an irresistible perfume. This is paradise . . .

In the sunny morning he is calling to his kids. My neighbor, Mr. Jay, father and husband, has returned to the daylight world.

Good morning, he says cheerfully. Good morning, I reply. Our smiles reveal nothing, but our eyes ask questions that only the night can answer.

After reading us the passage, Harriet looked up, paused, and with misty eyes asked, "Pretty, right? Oh, boy, I miss it. Shit."

ELLEN ADVOCATES FOR
A BETTER PRESENT

E llen says, "Being older does make life more intense, especially for someone like myself, who's always been like that. I used to have people stop me when I was ten years old and ask what bothered me, and I was just thinking intensely about something. I cannot conceive that you can live life without seeing its ironies, its necessary contrasts."

It's hard for Ellen, like Harriet, to shake the awareness that she's getting closer to the end of her life, but this awareness makes all of Ellen's experiences more vivid, especially her close relationships. As Ellen says, "The sense of having limited time, that keen awareness of the gift of the present, most certainly does affect the way Dolores and I are with each other physically and sexually. I feel like I'm sitting in front of a speedboat moving ahead into open space. Just feeling the strength of the wind against my face is the way that I feel about it, about my sexuality and my partnership at this stage of my life."

Ellen also directs much of her energy to her work. She teaches courses to train health aides and people working in nursing homes, sensitizing them to the fact that clients may be gay. She made this choice in response to her growing awareness that older people were going back into the closet because they feared being discriminated against. After years of denying her own homosexuality, Ellen is now determined not to have to hide who she is nor does she want any other older gay person to be put into that untenable position. "What has shaped my work now is the experience of knowing what it's like not to be comfortable in your own skin. I most certainly don't want to have to be in a nursing home hiding what is truly me."

TOO BUSY TO DIE:
FRANCES CELEBRATES LIFE

Many of the women we interviewed shared the sentiment that they shape their lives through their work and fortify themselves against loss through their creative passions. Frances told us, "What will my life look like in the next few years? The largest part of my life in the next few years is that I will die soon. On the other hand, I will never die, because, according to the name of my book, which will come out very soon, the name of the book is *Too Busy to Die*. And so I believe that I will never die nor do any of us ever die as long as we have been good to ourselves, if we've done good works for other people, our memories are with these people, and through these memories our spirit continues."

True to this belief, when Frances published her book, *Too Busy to Die*, at the age of eighty-seven, a year after David's death, she dedicated it to him. The dedication reads: *For David*

Steinberg, journalist and gentle man, sine qua non. She says, "Instead of missing David, let me celebrate David. I celebrate every bit of his body and of his mind."

LIVING FULLY TO THE END

L ife has twists and turns we can't predict, and riding that wave is an art form. We learned from Juanita's daughter, Wydenia, that Juanita, seventy-four, who seemed the picture of health and who had maintained a vital relationship with her boyfriend despite the dictates of her church, had advanced cancer. Within six months she died. We spoke with Wydenia shortly after. She was grief-stricken and her face was drawn until we asked her how she felt about her mother's vibrant sexuality. A smile crossed her face, and she perked up. Wydenia told us, "We had this conversation while she was sick in the hospital within the last six months concerning her sexual activities, and that sparked her up, that woke her up." Wydenia said with pride, "My mother lived until she died."

9.

AGING, THE GREAT ADVENTURE

It's easy for us to write scripts for our lives when we're young, imagining that this is the narrative we'll want to live out forever, but as our interviews showed us, interests and options often change with time. As the average life span of women and men continues to increase, it's becoming more and more common for people to take stock of their lives as they age, realizing that they aren't the same person they were twenty or thirty years earlier; that what they want now is different from what they wanted when they were young, sometimes very different. The women we spoke to told us that as they've aged they've become more courageous, more able to admit when something no longer works for them, and more willing to take risks to go after what they want. For Shelley and Elizabeth, that meant realizing in their fifties that they were no longer happy in marriages they started in their twenties and ending them with the hope of finding a better life. For Marnie, seventy-six, it meant starting to ski competitively at sixty, doing it with passion for fifteen years, and then, in a quick about-face, realizing she wanted to get a master's degree in health coaching.

A friend asked to screen our documentary *Still Doing It* to celebrate her fiftieth birthday. In her speech to her gathered guests, she said, "I hope we're all 'still doing it,' whatever it is that turns us on as we get older, whether it's having lots of great sex, starting a new career, or running a marathon." Age gives us the time to rewrite the script of our lives, to go for things we always wanted or things we've just realized interest us. These plot twists can keep life thrilling.

FINALLY GOING FOR IT

Shelley, sixty-six, had been feeling for years that she wanted to do something to help the world. The mother of two grown sons, she has a full-time career as the executive director of an affiliate of the National Employment Lawyers Association. She has a house at the beach, a wide circle of friends, and a passion for staying in shape. Her life is full. But reading the paper day after day, learning about the plight of people in Africa, she felt she needed to do something in whatever way possible.

Nearly 60 percent of the women surveyed by ACCESS would be happy to stay the age they are now, and less than one-third of them would want to go back ten years and "do it all again."

The passion finally overtook her and in December 2007 she went to Tanzania, where she worked in an orphanage for kids whose parents have died of AIDS. The trip was not easy. "It was very physical, very hot, 90 to 95 degrees," and she shared a room with four other women. The oldest other volunteer was thirty-eight; most were in their twenties. But, Shelley says, "it was an amazing experience." Only one kid had HIV, but few of them are ever going to get adopted. As there are little or no supplies, Shelley would take a group of the children and use the few supplies at hand to do art projects. Shelley told us that the kids connect emotionally only for short periods of time, then seem to disconnect, knowing all too well that volunteers come and go. Only one little girl, Lucy, bonded to Shelley and Shelley fell in love with her.

It wasn't easy to leave, but she felt like she had been able to do something, to bring some joy to kids who have so little. "For those few weeks I feel like I made a difference. The poverty there is just unbelievable." And Shelley is now planning to try to fundraise to get basic supplies to the orphanage: "toilet paper, formula, diapers."

BEYOND THE FINISH LINE

Sometimes, however, plans change. At seventy-five Marnie was determined to win one more gold medal in ski racing, but a year later the landscape looked totally different to her. She had several trips planned: one with her grandchild, another for a reunion at her alma mater, Smith College . . . but suddenly, after fifteen years of racing, she thought, "Were I to get hurt it would really goof up what's on my plate, and what's on my plate is more important than my trying to get another gold medal. I mean, one gold medal is really enough; I don't have to get another one. And what if I went out there and didn't get one? I would be really upset. And I thought, 'I'm not going to do that. I haven't retired from skiing. I've just retired from racing. Racing is just a very, very big commitment of time, and I'm just choosing to spend my time doing other things.'"

Marnie took the passion she had for skiing and shifted it to her current pursuits: getting a master's degree in health coaching and also studying to be a feng shui consultant. "It's been one of the most interesting things I've ever done in my life. First of all I adore going back to school. I've gone back to school ever since I got out of Smith, but I never got credit for it. I've never had to do papers or bibliographies on Internet sites. So it's a whole new language. And my fellow students are absolutely fascinating.

"I had a conversation with a physical therapist who said he would be very happy to recommend me once I get the certificate. And I've been doing this for free for him for twenty years. He'll say Mrs. Jones broke her ankle and she isn't doing x, y, z. You've had ankle issues. Would you talk to her? So I talk to her. So it isn't as if it's brand-new. I just haven't done it on a regular basis, nor have I charged money before. I find it absolutely fantastic. I just love every second of it.

"A whole lot of my friends my age play bridge at the country club, and that's life. Well, I don't feel that way. I want to do a whole lot more with my life than play bridge at the country club." When we asked Marnie how she maintains such an intense level of energy in everything she's involved in, she answered, "If you had to sum up how to age gracefully the one word would be *attitude*. Y'know, shit happens to everybody, but how do you handle it? My husband died three years ago. I went to a grief group. The same people are sitting around the same table, two, three, four years later still grieving the loss of their spouse. I grieved the loss of Carl, too. But I'm not going to do it once a week for three years."

Marnie's energy and openness have translated into her sexual life as well. She told us with glee, "I've got a brand-new beau. On the third of March my 166,000-mile Subaru died at a dangerous intersection, and I was directing traffic around my car that's died. Finally get that taken care of, and it's Lent and my daughter is running something at our church called Surprise Me, God. There is a book, and you read a chapter from it, and then you fill out the journal about how God has surprised you. So our church is having four different Sunday night suppers with table leaders, and Tami, my daughter, asked me to be one. So since I don't have a car now, my other daughter picks me up, and the whole way to the church I say, 'I hate car dealers. They don't like women. They don't like gray-haired women. They screw you out of five grand because they don't think you know any better,' and I went on and on. And I said, 'Which guy in the family do you think would be the best for me to take because I've got to replace this Subaru?'

"So we arrive at church. I've been going to this church for almost fifty years. I know 75 percent of the people, but there's a guy I don't know in the lobby, so I'm introduced. Well, this guy is at my table. I never lay eyes on him till five minutes earlier, and I thought, Well, sit down next to him to make him feel welcome and chat. So I do, and I look at him and I say, 'What do you do?' He said, 'I'm a car dealer.' I said, 'Oh my goodness. Surprise Me, God hasn't even started!' To make a long story short, I got a Chevy HHR—it's like a PT cruiser, only peppier—and now I'm dating Andy.

"This is the third boyfriend I've had since my husband died, three years ago. The first was one of my orthopedic surgeons. He was forty-nine and I just love him to death, but we were looking for different things. I want a playmate; he wanted a partner. There's a difference. Number two was very attentive at the start, but things kind of fizzled out. And finally the last time I saw him we were outside of my house, and he said, 'You probably think I'm weird.' I said, 'I don't think you're weird. Why would I think you're weird?' And he said, 'Well, I'm still kind of interested in the woman who dumped me ten years ago.' And I looked at this guy, and I said, 'Can I make a suggestion?' [*He looked at me, and I said,*] 'Therapy.' I closed the car door, walked into the house, and that was the end of that. [She laughs.] I mean, get a life, buddy. I mean, ten years ago.

"And now I'm seeing Andy. I'm taking him for the first time Saturday night to a birthday party for my ski team. He's met my family, but it's the first time my peers, my peers being people in their fifties—everyone on my ski team is in their fifties—with their husbands will meet him. I'm looking forward to that. It's been fabulous. He's sixty. That beats forty-nine. One of my kids was freaked out because I was one year younger than my forty-nine-year-old boyfriend's mother.

"Andy's [only] sixteen years younger. I certainly would never ever go out with someone unless he was younger, because I looked after Carl, who was fifteen years older than me, for five years. I've been there, I've done that, and I'm never doing that again. I mean, I met a guy in Cleveland who wanted me to go with him to Thailand. And he was wealthy and attractive and nice. And I looked at him, and I said, 'That's so sweet, but I've been to Thailand. Thank you, anyway.' The guy was eighty-five. Not doing that. I don't care who you are. Not doing that.

"Andy loves to ski and he has a lot of energy, and we just connected. I mean, "Surprise Me, God" is exactly what happened. And I'm just wild about my car, and I just think he's a whole lot of fun, and that is all I am looking for. He's getting divorced and could be looking for more down the line, but at the moment he's not, and who knows what down the line holds for anybody?"

PASSION

Becky, sixty, told us that passion has always been the driving force in her life. "For me it motivated my choice of careers, the things I've done and tried to do in my life. It was marrying my second husband, and retiring early to do photography full-time. If you're losing passion, you have to figure out what you need to do to get it back."

Before Becky retired, she set up programs for people with disabilities that encouraged the creative expression of the people who were enrolled as well as that of Becky and the other coordinators. She remembers the success of a weaving program that she developed: "It became the passion of so many people. It became something brand-new that they could do, with a tangible product. The group still operates. We've sold to boutiques all around the country—and that's an important connection—somebody else thinks it's beautiful enough to buy. It fuels those flames. That was in 1995, and the program is still there. I ran into one of the women the other day. She's teaching another kind of weaving where they paint the warps. And she went on for ten minutes about painting the warps! It's the passion that doesn't have to leave if there's still something good and new to learn."

Photography has become the center of Becky's life. "I really like people and street photography and portraiture. I had a project last winter that I did where I had to tell a person's story in six photographs, and I chose the artist [James] De La Vega. I don't know if you know him. He's an artist in the East Village, so I was in his shop for six weeks. And it was amazing that I was so passionate about telling this story. It was all that I thought about. I went to sleep thinking about what pictures I was going to take. I took over six hundred pictures, and from that I had to pick six that somehow told his life best. And I just had a great time. I thought I nailed it. I thought I told his story. He did, too."

TRICKS FOR LIVING WELL

Betty, seventy-eight, knows that what turns you on is a very individual thing. "You have to beat your own drum, find your own song, get your own voice." But while everyone's taste is different, Betty also thinks that there are some universal tricks to living a fulfilling life. The first is having fun, no matter what. "It's the essence. If you can't laugh and have a good time, if there aren't those moments, why bother?"

When Betty advocates for the importance of laughing and having fun in life, it isn't out of a prosaic notion of eternal sunshine. Instead, her recognition of the importance of pleasure and freedom are at the core of what she feels we all need to be creative, fulfilled people. Betty has always been passionate about women's rights and political freedom, but after a lifetime of trying to keep the sexual revolution spinning, she is discouraged by the rise of Christian fundamentalism in the United States.

"After a lifetime of teaching and working and then finding out that now we're in a political climate where it's all being pulled out from under us is really difficult. The little tight-lipped Christians, and Bush and his cronies, and the whole thing that's gone on in our government is that these people are not having any fucking fun and pleasure in their lives, and they're going to see to it that you don't either. It's real mean-spirited and dangerous. And the thing of it is that it's more like a facade; I mean, a lot of these fundamentalists, we know that they're hiring prostitutes and using porn and jerking off. I mean, they're part of the consumers of sexual entertainment and they're vehemently against it, and [they say that it's] to protect the children. But, once again, it has nothing to do with the kids. They really want to wage war on sex, that's the whole religious approach. You know, make something prohibited and people are going to do it anyway, and now you've got them by the short hairs. Guilt. Manipulate them with guilt and fear."

Betty feels that people's creative skills should be encouraged as much and as early as possible so that people can follow their own passions, instincts, and interests to let go and really have fun. "If you haven't lived a childhood of exploration and experimentation and, you know, looking and curiosity and creativity, it's just going to get worse as you get older. So it starts early."

Betty continues to be surprised and exhilarated by the places her own life is taking her. Just like every other area of her life, her relationship with Erik has been a transforming adventure. As Betty explains, it's been yet another occasion to break all her personal rules. "I was sixty-nine when he first came, and it was right at the new millennium. We were going into 2000, and I was sure that everything was going to fall apart. And I just got it. After we were halfway into the first year of the millennium, I just got it.

Break all your rules, whatever rules you have, let it go. I am evolving, and I've learned a lot of lessons, and I am very, very clear that I'm a better person today than I was ten years, twenty years, thirty years, forty years ago, and that learning process continues. It doesn't stop."

TRAVELING

Elaine, eighty, says, "I'm not one of the people who says, 'Oh, gosh, I wish I was twenty-five or I wish I was thirty-five. I don't want to go back there. I really don't. In fact, some of my best days have been since I've gotten older." For her, fun and adventure means traveling wherever she wants. "I did one of my lifelong dreams. I wanted to see our United States! So I planned a trip to go across country, stopping at certain places, sleeping in a hotel, touring that place, and then going on to the next. I did that for fifteen days on Amtrak. Alone." When we asked if she had been scared she told us emphatically, "No! Oh, my God, I thought my family would go bonkers. They said, 'You can't go alone!' I said, 'Why can't I go alone? I'm healthy. I'm fairly intelligent.'

"My travel agency arranged everything for me. I paid for everything before I left here. My first stop was Albuquerque, New Mexico. And then I went on to Flagstaff and then to the Grand Canyon. Oh, my God, that was awesome! Honestly, if you don't believe in God, you gotta go to the Grand Canyon. I went to Salt Lake City, Utah, because I wanted to hear the Mormon Tabernacle Choir sing. You can't go to their service if you're not a Mormon, but you can go to their rehearsals. Three hundred voices in the choir—I've got goose pimples just telling you about it! It was just wonderful. And the structure of their building! And I'll tell you, I think I only saw one other black person. They have no black people in Salt Lake City, Utah!"

We asked Elaine if that made her uncomfortable. "No, not at all. At the hotel, I had one lady walk up to me and ask me if I was maid service. Oh, I thought that was funny. I just kind of chuckled and said, 'No, I'm not. I'm traveling, just like you are.' That set her back a notch. She was polite, but she was flabbergasted. . . . I got the biggest kick out of that.

"I had wonderful fun. I ended up in San Francisco. This was in August, and I thought I was going to freeze to death. I met wonderful people. In fact, I traveled on the train with a lady, and she and I are still writing to each other. She lives in Oregon, and she'd love to have me come out. She was a white lady, my age, doing the same thing, we were just going different directions. When we parted ways we exchanged contact information. I called her in Oregon, and she called me on my birthday. And we continue to keep in touch."

For Cara, sixty-six, traveling is also one of her great joys. It's a wonderful metaphor for the liberation she feels now after years of struggle—first hiding her homosexuality when she was a Mormon and then fighting with her ex-husband over custody of their kids. "I see a culmination of a lot of struggles and ambiguity and self-discovery. I see myself finding myself, accepting myself. I see it happening now in my sixties. And I see the future as a very wonderful thing because I see it as a time of less struggle, less confusion, less self-doubt, less worrying about the past and all that stuff.

"I just got back from Machu Picchu. I've been retired for a

year now, and seeing Machu Picchu, that was the highlight, that was my big trip, that was my dream trip. And it was wonderful. And part of it was because it was exhilarating to know that I'm in great health. We climbed, we did the mountains, and we were at twelve thousand feet. We went to Lima and Cuzco and Machu Picchu and all those places. We went to a school way up in the Andes mountains and visited with Inca schoolchildren. Oh, it was a wonderful, wonderful trip. And it was just the first of many, I hope. I want to go to Budapest, Hungary. This is my background. My mother's side of the family comes from there, and all three of my girls are interested in their heritage, so I'm very interested in going there and to Vienna and Prague. So that's what I'm thinking. That's my travel goal now."

CELEBRATING

Many women we interviewed celebrate the adventure of living by marking their birthdays with rituals. Elizabeth, seventy-four, considers her birthday an important occasion to commemorate her choices and accomplishments. She started the tradition ten years ago, when she renamed herself. "My last name, Amanecer, is a chosen name. After my divorce, I didn't want to keep my married name (Grosch), and my maiden name was Blough, and neither one of them had a pretty sound to them, so I picked the Spanish word for 'dawn' and had a naming ceremony at Esalen (a center for humanistic alternative education) and had it legally changed ten years ago. I considered it a spiritual experience to choose my own name."

Every five years she honors her birthday in some way by performing a ritual on her body. "I shaved my head for my sixty-fifth birthday when I was at Esalen. . . . a real cleansing experience and a ritual I recommend to all for their sixty-fifth birthday! For my seventieth birthday, I got a tattoo . . . just a little dragonfly on my shoulder, but it was something I wanted to do. Now as I approach seventy-five in a year, I am looking for something special to do. Any suggestions?"

Marnie also got a tattoo to celebrate her age. "I was sixty-eight when I did it. I had a friend, and she said, 'What are you doing on your birthday?' And I said, 'Well, Carl's going to take me out to dinner.' And she said, 'That sounds boring.' And I said, 'I couldn't agree with you more.' She said, 'I'm taking you to get a tattoo.' And I got an angel on my right butt, my right hip. And whenever I ski, that angel is protecting me. Isn't that funny?"

All of Marnie's grandchildren love the tattoo. One grandchild, a twenty-two-year-old graduating from St. Thomas, was even inspired to copy her. Justifying his barbed-wire tattoo to his mother, he said, "Well, Grams got a tattoo."

We actually met Tamara, sixty-nine, after we spotted her and noticed she had a tattoo. Having already spoken to Elizabeth and Marnie, we went up to her to ask if getting a tattoo was to commemorate a particular birthday, and she told us in fact it was. "I just remember when I turned sixty-five I thought, I need to do something to mark this year. And that's when I decided I would get a tattoo. Other people take trips, they throw big parties. We never gave big parties in our family, and I thought I would get a tattoo. My daughter had a few, and one of my sons had one. And I thought, That's a great thing to do."

It took Tamara almost a year to come up with something she felt would truly be celebratory. "I decided to use my granddaughter's name. And I thought, What a fabulous word to have on my arm. Everyone's going to question me, and they still do. I designed it because I'm a sucker for art, but it was fantastic. And it's meaningful to me because it's her name. People think maybe I'm a musician. I always wonder if maybe people think I'm a holy roller because it's a very religious kind of word. And I always tell people it's my granddaughter's name, and that's very joyful to me."

Tamara says if she has another grandchild she'll definitely get another tattoo. Meanwhile she's reveling in her life, which she says is the best it's ever been. "My mother seemed old when she was much younger than I, and sick. I remember in my childhood thinking that older people are old. I didn't have role models of people, especially women, who were older and fabulous."

A WHOLE NEW CHAPTER

Despite a culture that equates aging with decline, many older women told us that their creativity has heightened with age. Harriet has always written, but when she retired with a pension after thirty years of teaching she was finally able to give writing her full attention. And her recent struggles with aging have actually fueled her material, making writing more and more central to her life.

So it was a wonderful boost to her life and her new career when her book *Notes of a Nude Model* was published. She told us, "The publication of the book has given me a tremendous kick and really like a shot of something wonderful. Not having a lover and missing it somehow has been helped a lot by the fact that the book is a reality, and I feel very solid about it."

When we asked her what excited her the most in her life, she told us without hesitation, "Writing. Especially working on something new. Like this piece I'm doing right now on my father. Makes me feel wonderful, makes me feel really good. Thank God for the fucking computer because that really is keeping me from being depressed. I really feel being depressed is a surrender to all the worst things in life, and I hate it. Y'know, as long as I'm alive, baby, I'm not going to waste my time being depressed. And writing I connect to something really important in myself. I feel very whole when I write."

For Harriet, the writing process itself is infused with sensuality. "I love the computer because it seems alive. Much more than a typewriter. It's so sensitive. It's so responsive. I turn it on, and it says, 'Welcome.' I love that. And then if I'm lucky it will say, 'You've got mail.' [Laughs] I think that's swell, don't you? Especially if you live alone, it's really nice. There's something about it. Just being able to manipulate the words, to be able to change and mold them is wonderful. And it's so unbelievable if you've spent your whole life on a typewriter."

As Harriet has discovered, the thing that makes our heart race with excitement might change over time but nonetheless keeps it pulsing. As Harriet put it, "I mean, it's not an orgasm. But it's pretty damn good." And after feeling "so deprived," Harriet had a sudden turn of events in her sex life. Her ex-lover, twenty years her junior, who has been living in Cairo, called her when he was in town. After years of not seeing him, and not having sex, she told us, the chemistry was right there. "Baby, we fucked and it was wonderful."

At eighty, no longer interested in being involved in the day-to-day operations of her sex shop Eve's Garden, Dell also wrote a whole new chapter in her life. "I became an interfaith minister because I wanted to encourage people to see the connection between sexuality and spirituality. I want people to see sex not as a 'sin,' as our culture sees it, but to see it as sacred. Having sex should be a spiritual ritual. Your partner is a god or goddess, and seeing sexual relations as a sacred activity is what Tantric sex is all about. Too many people see it as no more than a physical act, y'know, let's just get off fast. But it's like a meditation in a sense, one of the most sacred experiences two people can have." Dell now gives talks at women's groups and centers. Encouraging people to see the profound link between their sexuality and spirituality has become her latest mission.

SINGING THE TRUTH

We went to see Lainie, sixty-six, sing at Joe's Pub in New York City. Onstage her earthy sensuality took hold of the multigenerational audience, her humor and playfulness as riveting as her powerful voice. Like Dell and Harriet, Lainie feels that her sexuality comes through in everything she does. "I think sexuality is in the very cells of your body. It's in the way you think. It's in the way you approach life, in the way you look at it. It's sensuality. It's not sexuality. It's sensuality. Everything about life is, if you're really and truly alive, if you really have that feeling somewhere in your solar plexus, then it comes through as making you appear and feel sensual, and in that way making you appear young. When you stop being sensual, I think, is when you start getting old. It doesn't have to be about sex. It has to be about life itself." For Lainie, being fully, sensually alive has always been about singing, and she's always felt that self-expression improves with age and experience.

When we asked her about her career goals, she told us a story about blues singer Alberta Hunter, one of her earliest heroines. "Alberta Hunter was a big star in the 1940s and sometime in the 1950s. When she was fifty-five years old, she left the business and the business left her, and she went and lied about her age and ended up being a nurse. Somebody, the son of a patient, recognized her, and phone calls were made, and by this time she was in her seventies! Because the lying about her age meant that she didn't retire when she should have retired, she was still working there when she was seventy-plus. Suddenly her whole career was restored to her.

"I saw her at The Cookery when she was eighty-two or something. Her dressing room was at the other end of the restaurant, so she had a rather long walk of it to where the bandstand was, and she just really kind of shuffled. But she got to the microphone and she had these long red fingernails, and she planted herself in front of it and just sang from the middle of her belly. She sang 'The Glory of Love': 'You've got to give a little, take a little, let your poor heart break a little, that's the story of, that's the glory of love.' And she sang it with the kind of truth that you only have when you're eighty years old. And I just wept. It was so extraordinary. And, yes, that's what I want to be able to do. I want to be able to sing in front of a microphone when I'm eighty years old and have people know that I'm telling them the truth. I'm singing the truth. That's all I want to do. I want to sing the truth."

Marnie told us, "The twenty-eighth of July I'm jumping out of an airplane." When we asked her why, she replied, "Because I want to! I've been teaching aerobics for twenty-two years, and my three best friends are all in their early fifties, and we call ourselves the Ya-Yas, and we have dinner about every six weeks, and the Ya-Yas are all jumping out of an airplane. One Ya-Ya did it a year ago, and I saw this video of Carol jumping out of this airplane and I thought, y'know what? You could die from doing anything. I could walk out the front door and be killed by an automobile in the next hour. I don't want to miss anything. I want to make sure I've done everything that I can think of to do that's fun."

It was surprising to us how many of the women we interviewed spoke to us about wanting fun, wanting to laugh and enjoy life much more than they did when they were younger. Marnie told us, "I was one of those people who with one exception never got out of the box. If my parents said jump, I'd say, How high? I think I was extremely responsible. I mean, if my parents wanted me to go to Smith, I went to Smith. I didn't personally think, I'm going to Smith because I think it would be a hoot and a half. So I would say the older I get [the more I realize] you only have one chance, so you better do everything you want to do."

Clearly, women over sixty are already far more adventuresome than the media show. But as boomers age, changing jobs and lovers, reinventing the scripts of their lives in unique and exciting ways, having the time to assess one's life and transform it will increasingly be seen as one of the privileges of aging.

The secret isn't staying young forever, for that's a cultural fantasy we all have to acknowledge as illusory. But as Joyce, a filmmaker and psychologist, put it so succinctly, "We're here for whatever time, and it's finite. We have to live life as fully as possible and just soak in all that has to do with joy and pleasure. It's a vital life energy, and if we're fortunate enough to move the cobwebs away—because I think we all have to do that [throughout our lives]—and be in touch with and tap into that spark from the universe, then we'll always be turned-on people."

NOTES

1. http://64.23.76.120/NEWS/SeniorStats/6-03-09-Most Comprehensive Analysis.htm (2/13/2007).

2. U.S. Census Bureau, *65+ in the United States: 2005*, p. 38.

3. He, Wan, Manisha Sengupta, Victoria A. Velko, and Kimberly A. DeBarros, U.S. Census Bureau, Current Population Reports, P23-209, *65+ in the United States: 2005* (U.S. Government Printing Office: Washington, D.C., 2005), p. 147.

4. U.S. Census Bureau, *65+ in the United States: 2005*, p. 23.

5. *Ibid.*

6. Kathy Bosch, "Ageing Sexuality," NetFact blurb from *Family Life Education*. www.ianrpubs.unl.edu/epublic/pages/publicationD.jsp?publicationld =129.

7. *Ibid..*

8. All statistics taken from The Well Project. www.thewellproject.org/ womens_center/HIV_and_Older_Women.jsp.

9. Reuter's Health article. Source: http://preventdisease.com/news/articles/ exercise_cuts_breast_cancer_risk.shtml. Accessed on April 29, 2007.

INDEX